WORLD WAR II
TRIVIA QUIZ BOOK

VOLUME I: EUROPE & NORTH AFRICA

FORGOTTEN FACTS ABOUT
THIS CENTURY'S BIGGEST LAND GRAB

BY ERHARD KONERDING

MJF BOOKS
NEW YORK

Published by MJF Books
Fine Communications
322 Eighth Avenue
New York, NY 10001

World War II Trivia Quiz Book
ISBN-13: 978-1-56731-758-9
ISBN-10: 1-56731-758-8

Printed in the United States of America.

MJF Books and the MJF colophon are trademarks of Fine Creative Media, Inc.

QM   10   9   8   7   6   5   4   3   2   1

CONTENTS

Answers are located at the end of each chapter.

"Not in vain" may be the pride of those who survived and the epitaph of those who fell.

Winston Churchill

Weapons

Every bullet has its billet.

Prince William III of Orange

An incredible number of weapons were used in World War II, from commonly known tools of war such as the M-1 rifle, the German "88" artillery piece, the Spitfire fighter, and Sherman and Tiger tanks, to the many weapons and devices which were kept so secret that they are still not widely publicized. Even the weapons held by soldiers and sailors on many fronts have some obscure or surprising characteristics.

1. The portable Bailey Bridge, consisting of prefabricated steel girder sections, was named for its inventor, a (an):

A. Royal Canadian Navy officer
B. American professor from MIT
C. Australian engineer officer
D. British engineer

2. Ferdinand Porsche, best known for his postwar sports car designs, also created all but which of the following:

A. The amphibious military Volkswagen, Schwimmwagen (Typ 128)
B. The tank-destroyer "Elephant"
C. The Pzkfw V "Panther" tank
D. The original design for the "King Tiger" tank
E. The "Maus," (mouse), a 200-ton tank design

3. Only one Allied jet fighter saw operational combat service in World War II. It was the:

A. deHavilland Vampire F. Mk I
B. Bell P-59 Airacomet
C. Gloster Meteor F Mk III
D. Lockheed P-80 Shooting Star

4. Which of these standard army rifles has the largest caliber:

A. Enfield Mk. I (British)
B. Mauser Kar. 98k (German)
C. Garand M-1 (U.S.)
D. Mannlicher-Carcano (Italian)
E. Tokarev (USSR)

5. Which of these artillery pieces has the smallest caliber:

A. German 12 cm howitzer
B. British 25-pounder
C. U.S. M-1 105mm. howitzer
D. Soviet 100mm. antitank gun

6. More V-2 rockets were launched against this target than any other:

A. Brussels
B. London
C. Portsmouth
D. Antwerp

7. Hedgehog was the name for:

A. A German beach defense device of welded steel
B. An American concrete-busting armor-piercing shell
C. A British antisubmarine rocket system
D. A British tank trap devised by the Home Guard
E. A and C above
F. B and D above

8. The brilliant British inventor Barnes Wallis designed all but one of the following. Which was it?

A. The "Grand Slam" and "Tallboy" giant bombs
B. The geodesic Wellington bomber
C. The Dambuster bomb
D. The Mosquito plywood bomber
E. The R100 dirigible

Match the following secret weapons or devices with their functions:

9. __ Window
10. __ Oboe
11. __ Rebecca
12. __ Piperack
13. __ VT

A. A proximity fuse, which exploded near the target
B. An airborne radar jamming device
C. Strips of tinfoil to jam radars
D. Direction finding device used in conjunction with the S-phone
E. Range and direction-finding instrument system used by RAF bombers

14. German tanks used a distinctive numbering system. It consisted of:

A. One number superimposed above 3, all in a triangle; the top number was the individual tank number, the bottom 3 indicated the regiment, company, and platoon
B. Three numbers in red or white, or outlined in white or black; first number indicated company and battalion, second the platoon, third the individual vehicle
C. A chevron on the vehicle side: facing forward, backward, up or down to indicate company; stripes on the barrel to show platoon; and letters on the turret for individual vehicles

15. The bomb which nearly killed Hitler on July 20, 1944, was:

A. A modified Luftwaffe anti-personnel bomb
B. A British plastic bomb captured from SOE agents in France
C. A Wehrmacht land mine
D. A Russian sabotage device captured from Soviet partisans

16. The DeLisle Silent Commando Carbine Mk I consisted of:

A. An M-1 carbine with silencer and folding stock
B. A Sten Mk IV with silencer
C. A Lee-Enfield stock and action modified to fire .45 cal. rounds from a Colt pistol magazine, with silencer
D. A Mauser M-1896 9mm. pistol with shoulder stock and silencer

17. The "stuffed rat" was:

A. A typical meal for Russian prisoners in Germany
B. Rat skin containing explosive, planted by SOE saboteurs in coal bins, meant to explode in boilers
C. Nickname for a camouflage suit worn by snipers in Britain's Home Guard
D. The insulting name given to Hermann Goering by the Soviet editorial cartoonists

Wehrmacht armored vehicles were often named after animals, a practice continued by today's West German Bundeswehr. Can you identify each of the following German WWII armored fighting vehicles:

18. ___ Hetzer (harrier)
19. ___ Guderian Ente (Guderian duck)
20. ___ Moebelwagen (furniture truck)
21. ___ Brummbaer (grizzly bear)
22. ___ Nashorn (rhino)
23. ___ Hummel (bumblebee)

A. Quad 20mm. AA guns on Panzer IV chassis
B. 75mm. antitank gun on Czech T38 tank chassis
C. 75mm. antitank gun on Panzer IV chassis
D. 150mm. howitzer on Panzer IV chassis
E. 88mm. antitank gun on Panzer IV chassis
F. 120mm. howitzer on Panzer IV chassis

24. The Sturmgeschuetz, a German antitank vehicle with a heavy gun mounted in a fixed armored superstructure rather than a revolving turret, was the idea of:

A. General Heinz Guderian
B. Field Marshal Erich von Manstein
C. Field Marshal Hermann Goering
D. Adolf Hitler

25. *Rasputitsa* is the Russian name for:

A. The "scorched earth" policy
B. The rainy, muddy season of Autumn
C. The machine gun
D. The marshy area south of Leningrad

26. The Soviets used dogs laden with explosives to destroy German tanks. These dogs:

A. Were successful, but the need for dogs to carry messages and first aid supplies was more urgent
B. Were shot by the Germans before they could near the Panzers
C. Tried to crawl under the familiar-smelling Russian tanks they were trained with
D. Were eaten by the underfed Russian troops they were sent out among
E. B and C above

27. The crude and cheap, yet effective, 9mm. submachine Sten gun used widely by British forces, was named for:

A. Its designers, Messrs. Stephenson and Enderby
B. Its designers, Shepperd and Turpin, and the Royal Small Arms Factory at Enfield
C. Its typical stentorian noise
D. The Belgian cities of Steenkirk and Enville, where the design originated

28. The fast tank designs of J. Walter Christie, brilliant yet mercurial American inventor, greatly influenced the design of the:

A. British cruiser tank series
B. Soviet BT tanks and the T-34
C. The German Panzer IV and its variants
D. The M4 Sherman tank
E. A and B above
F. C and D above

29. The Malcolm hood and Galland hood (also called ERLA Haube) were, respectively, British and German solutions to a similar problem. These hoods were:

A. Attached to winter uniforms in Arctic areas to greatly add to their warmth and comfort
B. Improved tank gun mounts to improve ballistic protection and eliminate "shot traps"
C. Newer engine covers for trucks to improve ventilation and rain water runoff
D. Curved, streamlined cockpit canopies which improved pilot all-around vision

30. Of the 22 million jerry cans (5-gallon cans) furnished to the Allied armies in France from June to August, 1944, how many were lost, stolen, or destroyed by the end of August:

A. One-tenth
B. One-fifth
C. One-third
D. One-half

31. The Fairbairn-Sykes commando knife widely used by Royal Commandos, which was manufactured by Wilkinson and other British cutlers, was designed by:

A. Two British surgeons, who advised commandos on the most lethal use of the knife
B. Two British colonial officials who had studied Chinese martial arts
C. An Oxford professor of anatomy and one of his prize pupils
D. Two cutlery experts at the Wilkinson factory

32. The "combat box" was:

A. A portable pillbox, made out of concrete and steel
B. A staggered, tight flight formation of B-17's
C. The wooden container in which C-rations were packed
D. A parachute container dropped to OSS agents in France

33. German anti-aircraft and anti-tank gunners kept track of their score of "kills" by:

A. Marking silhouettes of the destroyed tank or airplane on the gun shield
B. Carving notches in the tires
C. Painting stripes on the gun barrel
D. Hanging streamers from the gun shield

34. The expression "50-mission crush" used in the Army Air Forces referred to:

A. A psychological syndrome, similar to "battle fatigue" suffered by pilots and other aircrew
B. The appearance of the typically wrinkled AAF uniform
C. A style of mashing one's hat to look as if it had been through many combat missions
D. The hug that crew members ritually gave one another after surviving 50 missions

35. The Chrysler multibank engine was:

A. A multiple-row radial aircraft engine experimentally installed in the prototype B-19 bomber
B. An enormously powerful engine intended for the Dodge 10-ton transporter truck
C. A turbine engine used in several classes of landing craft
D. 5 automobile engines on a common crankshaft, mounted in many Sherman tanks

36. The M1 "steel pot" helmet standardized for U.S. Army use in 1941:

A. Used the crown design of the British-style M1917 helmet, with the rim removed and side and rear pieces added
B. Consisted of two parts: the 2.3 lb. steel shell and the separate 11 oz. liner with strap and suspension
C. Was designed with the help of the Metropolitan Museum of Art in New York City
D. Was redesigned in 1943 with a special release on the strap which separated when pressure on the strap was so great as to cause injury to the wearer
E. All of the above
F. A and B only

37. The plywood deHavilland Mosquito bomber used by the RAF and Commonwealth air forces was:

A. Used in low-level daylight precision attacks on selected targets
B. Capable of carrying 4,000 lbs. of bombs from England to Berlin and returning
C. Used as a pathfinder aircraft, and in "spoofing" attacks on bombing raids
D. Also employed as fighter-bomber, night fighter, and anti-shipping aircraft
E. All of the above

38. These Navy men are:

A. Trying out a one-man amphibious landing craft, which was never put into service

B. Examining a captured German remote-control explosive vehicle, which was intended to help foil Allied landings

C. Testing the scale model for the proposed armored landing craft, the "Alligator"

D. Checking out the British "Beach Clearance Vehicle, Remote Control," used to explode breaches in beach obstacles

Weapons Answer Key

1. D	9. C	17. B	25. B	33. C
2. C	10. E	18. B	26. E	34. C
3. C	11. D	19. C	27. B	35. D
4. B	12. B	20. A	28. E	36. E
5. B	13. A	21. D	29. D	37. E
6. D	14. B	22. E	30. D	38. B
7. E	15. B	23. F	31. B	
8. D	16. C	24. B	32. B	

People

Death and sorrow will be the companions
of our journey; hardship our garment;
constancy and valor our only shield.
We must be united, we must be
undaunted, we must be inflexible.

Winston Churchill

1. Noel Coward, assisted by David Lean, directed the classic 1942 movie
In Which We Serve. In the movie, Coward himself portrayed a fictional-
ized:

A. Captain Lord Louis Mountbatten and his ship, HMS Kelly
B. Admiral Henry Harwood and the HMS Exeter
C. Admiral Sir James Somerville and HMS Illustrious
D. Admiral Sir Andrew Cunningham, commander of the British fleet in
   the Mediterranean

Hollywood actors, both prewar and postwar, joined the armed forces in
various capacities. Match the following silver screen stars or directors with
their wartime careers:

2. ___ James Stewart
3. ___ Ronald Reagan
4. ___ Sterling Hayden
5. ___ Clark Gable
6. ___ John Huston
7. ___ Frank Capra

A. Air gunner on a B-17, saw com-
   bat tour over Europe
B. OSS officer in Italy and
   Yugoslavia
C. Filmed *Why We Fight* for the
   Army
D. AAF officer, never left USA
E. Bomber pilot over Europe
F. Made films for the Army, includ-
   ing *Battle for San Pietro* and
   Report from the Aleutians

British film stars and directors participated, too. Match:

8. ___ Leslie Howard
9. ___ Anthony Quayle
10. ___ Noel Coward
11. ___ Alfred Hitchcock
12. ___ David Niven

A. British intelligence officer on Gibraltar
B. Did counterintelligence work in South America
C. Directed 2 French-language films for Ministry of Information
D. Commando officer in Normandy and Germany, highly decorated
E. Lost when BOAC airliner was shot down by German fighters off France

13. William Wyler's Academy Award-winning 1942 film, *Mrs. Miniver,* starred Greer Garson in the title role of an Englishwoman during the Battle of Britain. Her husband was played by:

A. Walter Huston
B. Walter Pidgeon
C. Walter Brennan
D. Walter Slezak

14. Field Marshal Sir Bernard Law Montgomery often wore an Australian army bush hat adorned with the cap badges of the many regiments under his command. When he wore his beret, it had only two cap badges. These were:

A. Special Air Service and Scots Guards
B. Wessex Regiment and his Field Marshal's rank badge
C. Royal Tank Regiment and his Field Marshal's rank badge
D. Royal Army Ordnance Corps and 17/21 Lancers

15. Reinhard Heydrich, assassinated in Prague by 2 Czech patriots parachuted into Czechoslovakia by the British, was:

A. Chief of the Reichsicherheitshauptamt (RSHA)
B. "Protector" of Bohemia-Moravia
C. A Luftwaffe reserve fighter pilot
D. One of the architects of the "Final solution" to the "Jewish problem"
E. All of the above
F. B and D above only

16. Which of the following projects was the SS commando Otto Skorzeny *not* involved in:

A. Anti-resistance activities in Denmark
B. Infiltrating English-speaking German soldiers in U.S. uniforms behind American lines during the Battle of the Bulge
C. The canceled Operation Suicide, which proposed kamikaze flights in piloted V-1's
D. The "rescue" of Mussolini and his delivery to Germany
E. A failed attempt to assassinate the entire Red Army headquarters staff behind Russian lines
F. Rounding up conspirators in the failed Hitler assassination plot

17. Colonel Claus von Stauffenberg, who planted the bomb which nearly killed Hitler on July 20, 1944, had trouble placing the bomb properly, partly because of serious wounds he had suffered in North Africa. He had lost:

A. One eye
B. Most of his right arm
C. Three fingers of his left hand
D. His right leg below the knee, and his left foot
E. All of the above
F. A, B, and C
G. A, C, and D

18. Vladimir Peniakoff was:

A. A Russian field marshal executed by Stalin after failing to recapture the Crimean peninsula
B. Leader of "Popski's Private Army," a British LRDG group which harassed German forces in Africa and Italy
C. The highest-ranking Polish officer executed in the Katyn forest
D. A Soviet spy in Switzerland, member of the "Red Orchestra"
E. Captured Soviet general who led Russian forces fighting for the Nazi's

19. The last action in the European theater for which a Congressional Medal of Honor was awarded (to Raymond Knight) was:

A. An air mission over Italy
B. A ground action in Germany
C. An armored battle in Czechoslovakia
D. An infantry attack in Austria

20. Sir Frederick Arthur Browning, founder and leader of the British parachute forces, was married to the well-known writer:

A. Agatha Christie
B. Virginia Woolf
C. Beatrix Potter
D. Daphne du Maurier

21. General Omar Bradley was originally called "The Soldier's General" by:

A. Dwight Eisenhower
B. Field Marshal Montgomery
C. The correspondent Ernie Pyle
D. The cartoonist Bill Mauldin

The great number of air battles over Western Europe, Russia, Italy, and Africa produced many air aces (an ace has shot down more than 5 enemy planes). The top aces defeated many opponents, sometimes on more than one front. Polish, Czech, French, and other aces from captive countries scored some of their victories in RAF service. Match these leading aces with their number of "kills":

22. ___ Group Captain C.R. Caldwell (Australian)	A.	32 kills
	B.	33
23. ___ Wing Cmdr. Witold Urbanowicz (Polish-RAF)	C.	352
	D.	31⅓
24. ___ S/Ldr M.T. Pattle (South Africa)	E.	41
25. ___ Sgt. Josef Frantisek (Czech-Polish RAF)	F.	28½
26. ___ Flight Lt. George Beurling (Canada)	G.	38
27. ___ Major Erich Hartmann (German)	H.	20
28. ___ Group Capt. J.E. Johnson (RAF)	I.	31
29. ___ W/Cdr. B. "Paddy" Finucane (Irish)	J.	27½
30. ___ W/Cdr. C.F. Gray (New Zealand)	K.	28
31. ___ Col. Francis Gabreski (USAAF)	L.	62
32. ___ S/Ldr P.H. Clostermann (France)	M.	94
33. ___ Ivan Kozhedub (USSR)		
34. ___ Flt. Mstr. Eino Juutilainen (Finland)		

The sons of both President Franklin Roosevelt and former President Theodore Roosevelt fought in World War II, in Europe and the Pacific. Match FDR's sons with their service careers:

35. ___ Elliot   A. USMC officer in Pacific
36. ___ FDR, Jr.   B. Navy ensign in Pacific
37. ___ James   C. Naval officer at Operation Torch, later in
38. ___ John   Pacific
                       D. AAF general, though never pilot rated

Match TR's sons with their service careers:

39. ___ Archibald   A. Won Medal of Honor for Normandy action
40. ___ Kermit   B. Fought in the Pacific
41. ___ TR, Jr.   C. OSS member, and major in both U.S. and
                           British armies

42. Popular American bandleader Glenn Miller disappeared while flying aboard a USAAF aircraft. What type of aircraft?

A. A Douglas C-47 Skytrain
B. A Beech C-45 Kansan
C. A Convair C-87 Liberator transport
D. A Noorduyn C-64 Norseman

43. Moshe Dayan, later to be Israel's Defense Minister, was known for his black eyepatch. He had lost his eye:

A. During the invasion of Syria in 1941, while scouting for the British
B. In an accident while training as an RAF pilot in Southern Rhodesia in 1944
C. While fighting as a member of the Jewish Legion in Italy
D. While teaching British paratroopers at Middle East Parachute School at Ramat David airfield in Palestine

44. Antoine de St.-Exupery, author of the best-selling children's book *The Little Prince,* was, during World War II:

A. An officer of the French Foreign Legion in Africa and Italy
B. A leader of the Maquis in the Lyon area until captured by the Gestapo in 1943
C. A pilot in the French, and later Free French Air Force; lost on a combat mission
D. One of Charles de Gaulle's most trusted aides from 1941 on

45. Pierre Koenig, Charles de Gaulle's Foreign Minister in the 1950's, participated in World War II as:

A. French Foreign Legion officer in Norway in 1940
B. Foreign Legion officer in France
C. Free French general in North Africa, decorated for action at Bir Hakeim
D. A leader of the French underground
E. All of the above

46. The British scientist who assessed the bombing campaign on Pantelleria and then suggested the "interdiction plan" to destroy German transport behind the Normandy front, was:

A. Ronald Lewin
B. Solly Zuckerman
C. George Lindeman
D. Henry Tizard

47. Hans Ulrich Rudel received the Knight's Cross with Gold Oak Leaves, one of Nazi Germany's highest awards. He was a:

A. Tank commander on the Eastern Front with more than 200 enemy tanks to his credit
B. Stuka pilot who destroyed more than 500 Russian tanks, and several Russian warships
C. Paratroop leader who distinguished himself in Holland, Norway, and Crete
D. U-Boat captain who sank more Allied shipping than any other

48. The American newsman who scooped all his colleagues by several hours with the story of the French surrender to the Germans at Compiegne was:

A. Edward R. Murrow
B. Walter Cronkite
C. William L. Shirer
D. Harry Reasoner

49. Wing Commander Douglas Bader, RAF, was unique among British World War II aces because he:

A. Had also been an ace in the first World War
B. Had only one eye
C. Had lost both legs
D. Needed eyeglasses to see clearly

50. Four Army lieutenants received posthumous Distinguished Service Crosses, and a unique Special Medal for Heroism granted by the President and Congress in 1961, for an action that took place on the S.S. Dorchester on February 3, 1943. These men, Lts. Clark Poling, George Fox, John Washington, and Alexander Goode:

A. Replaced the dead Navy gun crew, then successfully fought off an attacking German raider, but were killed by gunfire from the German ship
B. Were the Catholic, Protestant, and Jewish chaplains who gave up their life belts to other men as the Dorchester sank
C. Rescued the engine room crew from the flaming interior of the ship, but died from smoke inhalation later
D. Organized efforts to throw the blazing cargo of volatile materials overboard, but were killed in an explosion

51. Conscientious objectors, who refused to become combat troops because killing others violated their religious beliefs, were imprisoned in World War I. In World War II, American C.O.'s:

A. Became chaplains' assistants
B. Joined the armed forces as medics or corpsmen
C. Were subjects of dietary and psychological experiments
D. Worked for forestry and soil reclamation agencies, even becoming "smoke jumpers"
E. A and B above
F. B, C, and D only

52. American servicemen stationed in England, Wales, Scotland, and Northern Ireland, often married local women. How many GI war brides came from the British Isles?

A. 30,000
B. 70,000

C. 110,000
D. 150,000

U.S. Department of Defense

53. This fighting man, photographed in Italy, is:

A. A Russian "Cossack" in German service
B. A member of the Italian "Foreign Legion"
C. An Indian Army "sepoy"
D. A French North African "goumier"

People Answer Key

1. A	12. D	23. H	34. M	45. E
2. E	13. B	24. E	35. D	46. B
3. D	14. C	25. K	36. C	47. B
4. B	15. E	26. D	37. A	48. C
5. A	16. E	27. C	38. B	49. C
6. F	17. F	28. G	39. B	50. B
7. C	18. B	29. A	40. C	51. F
8. E	19. A	30. J	41. A	52. B
9. A	20. D	31. I	42. D	53. D
10. B	21. C	32. B	43. A	
11. C	22. F	33. L	44. C	

Air Power

Keep 'em flying.

Slogan of the Air Forces,
poster caption, World War II

The use of air power in the second World War was on a far more massive scale than ever seen before. Both tactical and strategic air power appeared on most war fronts. Air superiority was the key to victory, from the Nazi blitzkrieg to ultimate Allied victory in the West.

1. Unarmed Luftwaffe He59 floatplanes painted white and marked with red crosses were used to rescue pilots downed in the English Channel. The RAF:

A. Gave these aircraft a wide berth, and made no attempts to harass them
B. Attacked them with its rescue vessels, in order to get to the downed pilots first
C. Shot them down after the "Red Cross" planes were seen suspiciously close to British convoys
D. Allowed these planes to overfly British soil to rescue German pilots who parachuted down in coastal England

2. The Regia Aeronautica, or Italian Air Force, participated in the Battle of Britain by:

A. Sending observers along on most German missions over Britain between December 1940 and March 1941
B. Providing antiaircraft gun crews for German bomber bases in Belgium and France
C. Furnishing fighter cover over Luftwaffe bases to protect returning bombers from British intruder aircraft
D. Sending 80 bombers and 98 fighters which attacked England from October to December 1941

3. The German bombing of Rotterdam while negotiations for surrender were going on caused great physical damage and:

A. 12 deaths
B. 800-900 deaths
C. 2,300 deaths
D. 10,500 deaths (estimated)

4. In the German conquest of The Netherlands, the Luftwaffe lost:

A. 2 aircraft, both to accidents
B. 42 aircraft, 18 to German flak
C. 75 aircraft
D. Over 525 aircraft

The many hundreds of British airmen who fought in the Battle of Britain were aided by other Allied pilots. For example, there were 23 each from South Africa and Australia, 7 Americans, 14 Free French, 11 Irish, one each from Palestine, Jamaica, and Southern Rhodesia. Match these Allied countries with the number of airmen who participated in the battle.

		Took Part
5. ___ Czechoslovakia		A. 104
6. ___ New Zealand		B. 94
7. ___ Belgium		C. 154
8. ___ Poland		D. 27
9. ___ Canada		E. 93

10. The Finnish Air Force, between 1939 and 1945, used aircraft produced in:

A. Britain, France, and Germany
B. Sweden, Finland, and The Netherlands
C. Italy, the U.S., and U.S.S.R.
D. All of the above
E. B and C only

11. The first air raid of the war comprising more than 1,000 bombers was:

A. The German raid on Coventry
B. The RAF attack on Cologne on May 30, 1942
C. The RAF and USAAF destruction of Dresden in 1945
D. The USAAF attack on Schweinfurt

12. The German special operations group KG200 participated in:

A. The Mistletoe (Mistel) piggyback aircraft project
B. Remote-controlled bomb tests
C. Secret flights using captured RAF and USAAF aircraft
D. Deep-penetration flights over Allied territory
E. All of the above
F. A, B, and C only

13. German air convoys of giant Me323's to and from Africa in waning days of the Afrika Korps:

A. Were a tremendous success, and served as an example for the later use of such convoys in Russia
B. Were savagely attacked and nearly wiped out by RAF, USAAF, and South African aircraft
C. Lost their way and had to return to Sicily more often than not
D. Were cannibalized as shelter and firewood by the Wehrmacht

14. The famous "shark mouth" insignia painted boldly on Flying Tigers aircraft in China were inspired directly by the design's previous use on their own P-40's by:

A. No. 14 Squadron, RCAF
B. No. 2 OTU, SAAF
C. No. 112 Squadron, RAF
D. The French Normandie-Niemen Regiment in Russia

1942 was a year of great aircraft production, though the number of aircraft produced continued to increase. Which nations produced which number of airplanes in 1942:

15. ___ Soviet Union	A.	23,670
16. ___ Germany	B.	40,000
17. ___ United States	C.	15,550
18. ___ Great Britain	D.	48,000

19. When, on May 23, 1944, Adolf Hitler ordered the Me-262 to be built as a bomber only, which of his subordinates said: "Any small child could see that this is no bomber but a fighter!"

A. Hermann Goering
B. Adolf Galland
C. Willy Messerschmitt
D. Erhard Milch

20. The Me-321 *Gigant* glider was converted to a powered air transport by the addition of:

A. 8 BMW VI engines with constant-speed propellers
B. 4 Junkers Jumo 211 engines
C. 6 Hispano-Suiza engines built in France
D. 6 Gnome-et-Rhone engines removed from French bombers

21. The prototypes of both the Me109 and Ju87 Stuka first flew with the same engine. This powerplant was:

A. The Rolls-Royce Kestrel
B. The Pratt & Whitney Wasp
C. The Junkers Jumo 210
D. The Daimler-Benz DB601

22. The armored ground attack airplane *Il-2 Shturmovik* was the most widely produced Soviet warplane. The USSR produced:

A. 15,000
B. 27,000
C. 36,000
D. 45,000

23. The Luftwaffe expression *"Flak nach vorn!"* (Flak up front) means:

A. Look out for the anti-aircraft fire in front of you!
B. Move the anti-aircraft guns up front!
C. Those guys in front are really catching a lot of flak!
D. Roughly, the equivalent of: "Damn the torpedoes! Full speed ahead!"

24. On March 31, 1944, 96 RAF bombers were downed on a raid over Nuremberg. This was remarkable because:

A. "Bomber" Harris doesn't mention it in his memoirs
B. This was even less than the expected losses
C. The city is not shown on historical maps of RAF wartime raids
D. The Luftwaffe used Me-262 jets as night fighters for the first time in this raid
E. A and C above
F. A and D above

25. The USAAF raid on oil refineries in the Rumanian city of Ploesti on August 1, 1943, is well-known and documented. The AAF also bombed Ploesti:

A. On June 11-12, 1942
B. On January 22, 1943
C. In April, May, and June, 1944
D. On December 11, 1944
E. A and C above
F. B and D above

The USAAF considered the Ruhr Valley the best-defended target in the Reich. The next two on the list were:

26. ___ 2nd place   A. Berlin
27. ___ 3rd place   B. Budapest, Hungary
                              C. Vienna, Austria
                              D. Ploesti, Rumania
                              E. Pilsen, Czechoslovakia

28. The 15th Air Force, based in Foggia, Italy, had a song which went as follows:

> "It's still the same old story,
> The Eighth gets all the glory,
> While we go out and die . . .
> The fundamental things apply,
> As flak goes by."

This song parodied:

A. As Tears Go By
B. The Years Go By
C. As Time Goes By
D. Bye, Bye, Blackbird

Pilots who scored victories over foes often decorated their own craft with "kill marks" to signify number of victories. Which air forces used which system:

29. ___ Luftwaffe   A. Miniature national insignia of downed air-
30. ___ RAF &   craft
      USAAF   B. Frontal silhouette of downed aircraft type,
31. ___ Soviet Air   later vertical bars, one pilot even using labels
      Force   peeled from beer bottles!
32. ___ Finnish Air   C. Miniature national insignia of *own* air force
      Force   D. Small vertical bar, often with miniature
                              national insignia of downed aircraft

33. Me109G-5 and later marks of that fighter aircraft were known as *Beule* ("bulge") to their pilots because of:

A. The awkward underwing gondolas containing MG 151 20mm. cannon, which hampered performance
B. The cowling bulge which covered the breech of the 13mm. MG 131 machine gun
C. The bulge in the top of the wing to accommodate the larger landing wheel added to those aircraft
D. The bulky under-fuselage mount for bombs or fuel tanks
E. The way the pilots bulged out of the too-snug seat

34. North American T-6 Harvard (Texan in U.S. usage) training planes delivered to Canada during the period of U.S. neutrality were:

A. First flown to Bermuda, where they were transferred to the RCAF, before being flown to Canada
B. Flown to the U.S.—Canadian border, then pushed or pulled across before being flown to bases
C. Given civilian serial numbers, and transferred to Canadian civil airports as "pleasure craft"
D. Crated, and shipped across the border as "farm equipment"

35. Air Marshal Sir Arthur Harris, architect of RAF raids on Germany, got the idea for firebombing cities of the Reich:

A. While watching London in flames from the roof of the Air Ministry during the German blitz
B. From watching an army demonstration of flame-throwers
C. After reading Dante's *Inferno* for the third time
D. From a serious fire at his country estate

36. The Russian "air blockade" used first at Demyansk and Kholm in 1942-43 was intended to:

A. Stop all German fighters from reaching front-line Russian troops
B. Prohibit German supply convoys on the roads
C. Prevent German air transport from supplying pockets of surrounded German troops
D. Strike at German supply lines hundreds of miles behind the front lines

37. Soviet pilots disliked the LaGG-3 wooden fighter plane (the predecessor of the more successful La-5 and 7), and said the LaGG acronym stood for:

A. "Wooden wonder plane"
B. "Aircraft guaranteed not to work"
C. "The German secret weapon"
D. "Lacquered guaranteed coffin"

38. The *Zwilling* (twin) was:

A. A double gun mount in the wing of a FW-190 fighter
B. Two Ju-52's towing a large glider
C. Two He-111's joined together with a fifth engine between, used to tow enormous gliders
D. A pair of jet engines in one underwing pod on the *Arado 234* jet bomber

German, British, and American parachutes used by airborne troops each had unique characteristics. Which of the following had which trait (Note: one number has two correct answers):

39. ___ U.S.
40. ___ British
41. ___ German

A. Could not be steered by the risers
B. The suspension lines opened before the chute canopy
C. The chute canopy opened first
D. Had a quick-release buckle which released the entire harness with a "smash" of the fist

42. These USAAF ground crew are rearming a:

A. P-38 Lightning
B. P-51 Mustang
C. P-47 Thunderbolt
D. P-39 Airacobra

Air Power Answer Key

1. C	10. D	19. D	28. C	37. D
2. D	11. B	20. D	29. D	38. C
3. B	12. E	21. A	30. A	39. C
4. D	13. B	22. C	31. C	40. B, D
5. E	14. C	23. B	32. B	41. A
6. A	15. B	24. E	33. B	42. C
7. D	16. A	25. C	34. B	
8. C	17. D	26. C	35. A	
9. B	18. C	27. D	36. C	

Naval Power

Sighted sub, sank same.

Donald F. Mason,
Radio message to U.S. Navy
Base, January 28, 1942

Unlike the war in the Pacific, the war in Europe was not one of hopping from island to island. Still, naval warfare was a major part of this theater of operations. The battle against the U-Boats, which sought to cut off England's vital supplies had to be won before the Allies could prevail elsewhere. Surface vessels, large and small, played roles on all fronts near large bodies of water. The amphibious landings in Africa, Italy, and France were the only way to get armies where they were needed.

1. The U.S. Navy captured the German submarine U-505 off the coast of Africa in early 1944. The sub was then:

A. Used by the U.S. Navy as the USS *Turbot* until it was lost in action
B. Lost while being towed, when the towing cable parted in mid-Atlantic
C. Briefly evaluated by the U.S. Navy, and towed to Chicago as a permanent museum exhibit
D. Turned over to the Free French Navy, and used by them until 1950, then scrapped

2. The *Schnorkel* device, used by U-Boats to supply air to crew and diesels while submerged, was a development of research begun in:

A. France
B. Norway
C. The USSR
D. The Netherlands

3. The *Bachstelze,* named for a German bird, was:

A. A powerless kite, driven by rotors, towed behind a U-Boat carrying an observer
B. A fake conning tower packed with explosives, towed behind a U-Boat to destroy any vessel which rammed it
C. A remote controlled missile launched by U-Boats to shoot down attacking Allied airplanes
D. An antiaircraft rocket towing a cable, used to entangle and destroy aircraft attacking U-Boat pens in France

Capital ships of the *Reichsmarine* were virtually all destroyed before the end of the war. Match each major German warship and its ultimate fate:

4. ___ *Tirpitz*	A. Scuttled off Uruguay, 1939
5. ___ *Bismarck*	B. Sunk in North Atlantic, 1941
6. ___ *Graf Spee*	C. Never completed, scuttled; salvaged by
7. ___ *Graf Zeppelin*	Russians
8. ___ *Adm. Scheer*	D. Bombed in Tromsofjord, 1944
9. ___ *Scharnhorst*	E. Bombed at Swinemunde, 1945
10. ___ *Luetzow*	F. Sunk off North Cape, 1943
(ex-*Deutschland*)	G. Scuttled at Gdynia, 1945
11. ___ *Gneisenau*	H. Bombed at Kiel, 1945

12. The Italian battleship *Roma* went to the bottom:

A. After being hit by a German air-to-surface missile
B. When torpedoed by an Italian submarine
C. When bombed by the RAF to prevent its use by the Germans
D. After an explosion of unknown origin amidships

13. The French battleship *Jean Bart* was:

A. Scuttled with the rest of the French fleet at Toulon on November 27, 1942
B. Put out of action by the USS *Massachusetts* during Operation Torch
C. Sunk by Royal Navy Swordfish torpedo planes at Mers-el-Kebir
D. At Martinique in the Caribbean when war broke out, and remained there until 1943

14. In 1941, the U.S. traded 50 World War I vintage destroyers to the British in exchange for bases in the Western Hemisphere. One of the destroyers, the USS *Buchanan,* was renamed HMS *Campbeltown;* its ultimate fate was:

A. Sunk as a blockship off Normandy in 1944
B. Packed with TNT, it was rammed into a German drydock at St. Nazaire, where it exploded
C. After ramming U-48, both ships sank together, with only 25 survivors
D. Donated to the Soviet Navy after being severely damaged while escorting a convoy to Murmansk

15. The Royal Navy Volunteer Reserve was dubbed the "Wavy Navy" because:

A. The officers waved rather than provide a proper salute
B. Inexperienced members took so long to get their "sea legs"
C. Their uniforms were usually terribly wrinkled
D. The rank insignia on officers' sleeves were "wavy" rather than straight

16. Kapitaen-Leutnant Guenther Prien:

A. Was the only survivor of the *Bismarck*
B. Sank HMS *Royal Oak* inside the Royal Navy base at Scapa Flow in 1939
C. Sank more merchant shipping than any other U-Boat captain in World War II
D. Was Admiral Doenitz's personal aide

17. Lothar Guenther Buchheim, author of the acclaimed novel *Das Boot* (The Boat) that was made into an award-winning movie, was, during the war:

A. A German war artist
B. Technical officer aboard a U-Boat
C. Captain of an E-Boat
D. A writer for the Propaganda Ministry

18. British wartime merchant marine shipping losses totaled:

A. 2½ million tons
B. 7½ million tons
C. 11½ million tons
D. 15½ million tons

19. Of 10,000 Norwegians killed in World War II, how many were merchant sailors:

A. 1,000
B. 3,000
C. 4,000
D. 6,000

20. After 1942, Allied naval superiority and long-range aircraft made the job of the U-Boats more difficult. How many U-Boats were sunk by Allied surface vessels:

A. 188
B. 246
C. 288
D. 342

21. Using the same numbers as above, tell how many U-Boats were destroyed by Allied aircraft (excluding bombing raids on submarine pens).

22. The "milch cow" submarines used to re-equip patrolling U-Boats at sea, and which were all rapidly sunk by the Allies, were designated:

A. Type VIII
B. Type XI
C. Type XIV
D. Type XVII

23. A general rule of thumb for submarine availability says that one-third of the boats are at their bases, one-third are en-route, and one-third are on station. On September 3, 1939, the *Kriegsmarine* had how many U-Boats:

A. 32
B. 57
C. 78
D. 101

24. The only U.S. battleships used in the European theater in 1944 were three older battleships which supported the amphibious landings in Normandy and Southern France. Which of these was *not* among them:

A. USS *Arkansas*
B. USS *Nevada*
C. USS *Florida*
D. USS *Texas*

A number of American destroyers became distinguished for a number of actions. Can you identify each "tin can"?

25. ___ USS *Pillsbury*
26. ___ USS *Reuben James*
27. ___ USS *Borie*

A. First U.S. warship sunk in WWII
B. Rammed U-405, both ships then sank
C. Crew members boarded captured U-505

28. After the North African invasion, U.S. submarines in the Atlantic:

A. Continued to operate from their Scottish base
B. Moved to the Caribbean to protect oil tankers there
C. Were sent to the Pacific, leaving the Atlantic for the Allies
D. Were transferred to the Mediterranean

29. The S.S. *Athenia* was the first British ship sunk by a U-Boat during World War II, on September 3-4, 1939. The German government:

A. Claimed full responsibility
B. Claimed that 3 Royal Navy destroyers sank the *Athenia*
C. Claimed that passengers on the *Athenia* saw a whale rather than a torpedo wake in the water
D. Claimed that the *Athenia* struck an iceberg
E. B and C above

30. American shipbuilders mass-produced a great number of Liberty ships to replace shipping lost to submarines. The average speed of a Liberty ship was:

A. 7 knots
B. 11 knots
C. 15 knots
D. 19 knots

31. The "Channel Dash" was a great achievement for the *Kriegsmarine,* in which the *Scharnhorst, Gneisenau,* and *Prinz Eugen* successfully left their Channel ports and reached the open waters of the Atlantic. This dash took place on:

A. Sept. 15, 1941
B. Feb. 12, 1942
C. May 6, 1942
D. Nov. 11, 1942

32. One method of countering German air attacks on convoys by FW 200 Condor bombers was by mounting catapults on merchant ships to launch:

A. Supermarine Spitfires
B. Grumman Martlets
C. Fairey Swordfish
D. Hawker Hurricanes

33. The smallest American aircraft to sink a U-Boat was:

A. An armed T-6 of the Army Air Force
B. A Navy F4F Grumman Wildcat from an escort carrier
C. A civilian light plane of the Civil Air Patrol
D. A Vultee Vindicator from Air Training Command

34. These U.S. Coast Guardsmen are:

A. Lowering sonar gear to listen for submarines
B. Preparing minesweeping equipment
C. Adding auxiliary fuel tanks to their vessel
D. Loading a depth charge on its launcher

Naval Power Answer Key

1. C	8. H	15. D	22. C	29. E
2. D	9. F	16. B	23. B	30. B
3. A	10. E	17. A	24. C	31. B
4. D	11. G	18. C	25. C	32. D
5. B	12. A	19. C	26. A	33. C
6. A	13. B	20. C	27. B	34. D
7. C	14. B	21. B	28. C	

Commandos
and Resistance

In war there is no second prize
for the runner-up.

Omar Bradley

Special forces such as the British Commandos and U.S. Army Rangers arose in World War II, as did the many anti-Nazi resistance groups in occupied Europe. Many of these groups had an impact far in excess of their numbers; others did not succeed. The bravery of both is undeniable.

1. The Germans, in their invasion of Holland, used which of the following deception techniques:

A. Germans dressed in Dutch uniforms to confuse the defenders
B. Dutch prisoners herded in front of German troops to prevent Dutch troops from firing on them
C. Both A and B

2. British "A" Force troops deceived Rommel before the El Alamein attack by:

A. Constructing a simulated fuel pipeline of gasoline cans
B. Covering tanks with "sunshields" to make them resemble trucks
C. Building a half-life-size railroad and terminal in the desert
D. Hiding artillery pieces in pits under trucks
E. All of the above

3. The Royal Army Commandos carried out their first large raid in March of 1941 on the Lofoten Islands in Norway. This raid resulted in:

A. The destruction of a Luftwaffe airfield used as a base to attack convoys, and the capture of a German general
B. The destruction of fish oil and fish meal factories, oil and gas tanks, and 11 small vessels, the recruitment of over 300 Norwegian volunteers for the Allied forces, and many Nazi and Quisling prisoners
C. The death or capture of most of the commandos when they were ambushed by the Germans, in a great setback for the commando movement
D. The destruction of a vital German radar base, and the return to England of many of its secret components

4. Orde Wingate, who had organized the Special Night Squads among Palestinian Jews in the 1930's, and who died in 1944 while commander of the Chindits in Burma, also:

A. Led Royal Army Commandos in raids on occupied France in 1942
B. Parachuted into France in 1941 in an unsuccessful attempt to organize resistance forces
C. Led "Gideon Force" to victory over the Italians in Ethiopia
D. Founded the British Airborne Divisions

5. General Robert Laycock, commando leader who tried to assassinate Rommel in Africa:

A. Was captured, then interrogated personally by Rommel. He later wrote *The Desert Fox* based on his experiences
B. Was unable to find the HQ and wandered for weeks with his commandos, striking targets of opportunity behind German lines
C. Was one of only two survivors of the failed attack, which struck when Rommel was elsewhere. Laycock and a sergeant spent two weeks in the desert with *The Wind in the Willows* as their only reading matter
D. Practically destroyed Rommel's HQ, wounded the Field Marshal, and then discovered a Luftwaffe airfield.

6. The raid on Dieppe, France, in August, 1942, by Canadian troops and British commandos was a costly operation, but provided Allied planners with important information for the planned invasion of the Continent. Of the 5,000 Canadians who participated, what percentage became casualties or prisoners?

A. 30%
B. 45%
C. 70%
D. 80%

7. General George Patton sent a force of 300 men toward the German prison camp at Hammelburg (where his son-in-law was held) to avoid a feared massacre. This force:

A. Was surrounded and destroyed by the Nazis before they reached the camp
B. Reached the camp, but were unable to free the prisoners and were forced to retreat
C. Liberated the prisoners, but were attacked and decimated on the return trip to American lines
D. Returned safely to Allied lines, but without Patton's son-in-law, who had been moved to another camp

8. The Denison smock was:

A. A roomy, camouflaged jacket worn by British paratroopers
B. A near-copy of the German paratrooper coverall, worn by British paratroopers
C. A leather jerkin worn over battle dress by most British soldiers in the field in cold weather
D. A coverall worn by Royal Tank Regiment troops in winter

9. U.S. Marines engaged in ground combat in Europe in small numbers. These Marines were:

A. Observers who landed with Royal Marine Commandos in early raids in Norway
B. Boat crew who came ashore at Normandy when their landing craft was sunk by enemy action
C. Crew of an antisubmarine PBT Catalina who ran out of fuel off France, swam ashore and joined the French Resistance
D. O.S.S. guerrillas who organized French resisters behind the German lines after D-Day

10. The first American ranger troops in World War II received special commando training at:

A. Achnacarry, Scotland
B. Camp Borden, Ontario
C. Brecon Beacons, Wales
D. Belfast, Northern Ireland

11. German parachute troops *(Fallschirmjaeger)* were mostly members of the:

A. Wehrmacht
B. Kriegsmarine
C. Waffen SS
D. Luftwaffe

12. The 1st Special Service Force, originally planned as a raiding force to operate in Norway, but which participated in combat in Italy and Southern France before being disbanded in late 1944, was made up of men of two nationalities. These were:

A. Australians and New Zealanders
B. British and South Africans
C. Americans and Canadians
D. British and Canadians

13. Soviet paratroopers were most often dropped in small numbers behind German lines to support partisan groups. Two exceptions to this practice occurred in January, 1942, when hundreds of Russian parachutists were dropped near:

A. Vyazma
B. Orel
C. Kharkov
D. Rostov

14. The favorite vehicle of the Long Range Desert Group in its early days was:

A. The British 3-ton 4-wheel-drive Austin K5 truck
B. The Daimler Mk. I Scout Car
C. A 30-cwt Chevrolet commercial truck, stripped down to reduce weight
D. The Canadian Dodge weapons carrier

15. The British commandos chose a forest green beret as their distinctive headgear, as did the U.S. Special Forces more recently. The first of these green berets were made by:

A. A distinguished London haberdasher
B. The official supplier to Canadian forces
C. A Scottish tam-o'-shanter maker
D. A Welsh hatter

16. General Draga Mihailovic was:

A. Leader of the Chetnik guerrillas in Yugoslavia
B. Josip Tito's second-in-command with the Yugoslav partisans
C. The puppet leader of German-dominated Croatia
D. The head of the Bulgarian government in exile in the USSR

Commandos and Resistance Answer Key

1. C	7. A	13. A
2. E	8. A	14. C
3. B	9. D	15. C
4. C	10. A	16. A
5. C	11. D	
6. C	12. C	

Acronyms,
Code Names and Slang

I have never met anybody who wasn't against war. Even Hitler and Mussolini were, according to themselves.

David Low

Military and wartime life engenders its own language, one which is often incomprehensible not only to civilians, but also to members of other services. Acronyms such as radar (RAdio Detection And Ranging) were widespread. Code names to preserve the secrecy of upcoming operations, or devices, proliferated as never before. Service slang serves to deflate the pomposity of military life and people, and to express deep personal feelings about war, life, and death.

1. The German dive bomber Ju87 was known by its acronym, *Stuka,* which is short for:

A. Stumpfkabelflieger
B. Stufenkampfgeraet
C. Sturzflugkarosserie
D. Sturzkampfflugzeug
E. Stundenkartefliegerei

Both Axis and Allies used code names for upcoming operations in order to preserve secrecy. Match each code name with its objective:

2. ___ Market Garden
3. ___ Bellicose
4. ___ Sea Lion
5. ___ Plate Rack
6. ___ Chastise
7. ___ Hercules

A. RAF air raid on Friedrichshaven
B. The aborted German invasion of Britain
C. The 1945 bombing of Dresden
D. The airborne landings in Arnhem and nearby
E. The "Dambusters" raid
F. The planned German invasion of Malta

8. *Gestapo* was the acronym for the dreaded and hated German:

A. Gesicherte Stabspolizei
B. Gemeine Staffelpolizei
C. Gefaehrliche Starkerpolizei
D. Geheime Staatspolizei

GI's in Britain, as well as the local civilians, often had trouble understanding the expressions used by their fellow English-speakers. What do these English expressions mean?

9. ___ Knock up
10. ___ Keep your pecker up
11. ___ Wash up
12. ___ Rubber

A. An eraser
B. Stay cheerful
C. Call on someone
D. Do the dishes

Army Air Forces slang was incomprehensible to many Americans, too, such as:

13. ___ Meat wagon
14. ___ Section 8
15. ___ Milk run

A. Psychiatric discharge from the service
B. Routine or easy bombing mission
C. Ambulance

Different classes of U.S. Navy warships were named for different people, places, or things:

16. ___ Battleships A. Major cities
17. ___ Battle cruisers B. American war heroes
18. ___ Cruisers C. States
19. ___ Destroyers D. Fish
20. ___ Submarines E. Territories

An enormous number of landing ships and landing craft were developed in World War II. While these were mostly employed in the Pacific, the landings in North Africa, Italy, and France required numbers of them, too. The acronyms for each of these types is a giveaway, so you will need to identify each type by its length in feet:

21. ___ LSD (Landing Ship, Dock) A. 25 ft.
22. ___ LVT (Landing Vehicle, Tracked) B. 457 ft.
23. ___ LCI (Landing Craft, Infantry) C. 50 ft.
24. ___ LSM (Landing Ship, Medium) D. 158 ft.
25. ___ LCM (Landing Craft, Medium) E. 200 ft.

26. A group of French resistance forces named themselves the *Maquis,* after:

A. The scrubby countryside of southwestern France
B. A marquis who was their early leader until captured, tortured, and killed by the Gestapo
C. The diamond-shaped insignia worn by them, copied from the divisional insignia of the French army in that area in 1940
D. The acronym for "fighting military men"

27. Lend-lease trucks, jeeps, and tanks delivered from the United States to the Soviet Union still bore their serial numbers with a prefix of "U.S.A." Soviet troops said the letters stood for:

A. "A gift from our American friends"
B. "Soviet-American friendship forever"
C. "Solidarity with American workers"
D. "Kill that son-of-a-bitch Adolf"

Secret and clandestine groups used acronyms, too. Match:

28. ___ OSS
29. ___ SOE
30. ___ FFI
31. ___ FTP
32. ___ SIG

A. Communist guerrillas in France
B. A small group of British commandos and German Jews used in North Africa, nearly all were killed on their only mission
C. American spy and sabotage group
D. French resistance group loyal to General deGaulle
E. British spy and sabotage group

Acronyms, Code Names and Slang Answer Key

1. D	8. D	15. B	22. A	29. E
2. D	9. C	16. C	23. D	30. D
3. A	10. B	17. E	24. E	31. A
4. B	11. D	18. A	25. C	32. B
5. C	12. A	19. B	26. A	
6. E	13. C	20. D	27. D	
7. F	14. A	21. B	28. C	

D-Day

The first and great commandment is,
Don't let them scare you.

Elmer Davis

The Allied landing on Normandy on June 6, 1944, better known as D-Day, was the long-awaited opening of the second front against the Nazis. U.S., British, Canadian, and other troops arrived in Normandy by parachute, glider, or landing craft. Both Allied and Axis forces had made preparations for the attack.

1. From May 5 to June 2, five code names for the D-Day operations appeared in the London *Telegraph* crossword puzzle. Their appearance prompted MI5 to investigate but coincidence rather than espionage turned out to be the answer to this "puzzle." Which of the following words did *not* appear in the *Telegraph?*

A. Overlord
B. Mulberry
C. Juno
D. Omaha
E. Neptune
F. Utah

2. The German forces under Field Marshal Rommel had prepared many unpleasant surprises for the invading Allies, including many obstacles on the beaches and landing fields. *Rommelspargel* ("Rommel asparagus") consisted of:

A. Ditches in plowed fields to prevent glider landings.
B. Poles planted in open fields to deter glider landings.
C. Poles planted in the beaches to rip up landing craft.
D. Sharpened stakes intended to impale paratroopers.
E. A fast-growing ground cover to camouflage landing sites.
F. Tainted crops in Northern France to poison the invaders.

The British General Hobart designed a number of specialized armored vehicles to defeat beach defenses. These "Funnies" equipped the 79th Armored Division of the Royal Army, but the U.S. forces saw no need for them, and had a harder time crossing the beaches. Can you match the name of each "Funny" to its purpose?

3. ___ Crab

4. ___ Duplex Drive
(DD)

5. ___ Bobbin

6. ___ Crocodile

7. ___ AVRE

8. ___ Ark

A. A device to unroll a canvas roadway over the sand.

B. An armored flame thrower.

C. Unfolding bridge girders on a tank, to allow others to pass over obstacles.

D. A tank made amphibious by addition of screw propellors and a raised canvas flotation screen.

E. A tank armed with the "Dustbin" spigot mortar (Petard), often also carrying fascines (bundles of brush used to fill in ditches)

F. A tank mounted with twirling chains in front intended to explode land mines

9. The 6th Airborne Division ("Red Devils") of the Royal Army used what instrument as a rallying signal upon landing?

A. A London bobby's whistle
B. An English hunting horn
C. An Irish pennywhistle
D. A snare drum

10. The U.S. airborne forces issued a device to individual paratroopers so they could recognize one another in the dark after dropping in Normandy. This device was:

A. A kazoo
B. A clicking metal "cricket" toy
C. A wooden duck call
D. A police whistle

11. The only Allied warship lost off the Normandy beachhead was the:

A. H.M.S. Warspite
B. U.S.S. Saginaw Bay
C. U.S.S. Corry
D. H.M.S. Botany

12. Theodore Roosevelt, Jr., son of the late President, begged his superiors for permission to land on Normandy. This was finally granted. General Roosevelt arrived on the beach and:

A. Was the first Allied general to be killed there
B. Was immediately wounded and sent to the hospital in France. He later distinguished himself fighting at the Siegfried Line
C. Was awarded the Medal of Honor for distinctive bravery in Normandy, given command of a Division, but died of a heart attack before assuming command
D. Was captured by the Germans and held prisoner until the liberation of his prison camp in Germany

13. The Luftwaffe attacked the landing beaches in the morning and evening of June 6, with, respectively:

A. 2 FW-190's and 6 Ju-88's
B. A squadron of FW-190's and 8 Me-109's
C. 3 squadrons of Me 262's and 4 FW-190's
D. 8 FW-190's and a mixed squadron of FW-190's and Me-109's

14. On the morning of the June 6th Allied invasion, Field Marshal Rommel, who had prepared so carefully, was:

A. At home in Stuttgart to celebrate Frau Rommel's birthday
B. In East Prussia, conferring with the Fuehrer
C. Asleep in his forward HQ in Le Havre
D. In Paris, meeting with Field Marshal von Runstedt

15. One of the devices tested for use in the invasion was the Great Panjandrum, a rolling pair of wheels propelled by rockets and containing two tons of explosives. When demonstrated before a high-ranking contingent of observers, the device ignominiously:

A. Headed out to sea, never to be seen again
B. Charged for the crowd, then headed to sea and exploded
C. Raced far inland, catapulted itself over a hill, and exploded in an abandoned village
D. Failed to move at all, and had to be disarmed by a team of bomb defusing experts at great risk

16. An elite force of American troops had the objective of the cliffs at Pointe du Hoc, where intelligence indicated that German gun positions threatened Omaha Beach. After scaling these cliffs at great cost, these men found the gun mountings empty. This intrepid band named itself after its colonel, and was called:

A. Rudder's Rangers
B. Rogers' Rangers
C. Merrill's Marauders
D. Hogan's Heroes

17. The 4th Infantry Division of the U.S. Army suffered the following casualties on D-Day:

A. 12 killed, 185 other casualties
B. 52 killed, 388 other casualties
C. 152 killed, 208 other casualties
D. 575 killed, 2,100 other casualties

18. The 2nd SS Panzer Division *das Reich* was harrassed by both Allied air forces and French partisans on its way to Normandy from its base in Toulouse in southern France. The division finally arrived near the front in full force on:

A. June 15
B. June 22
C. June 27
D. June 30

and began actual combat on:

A. June 18
B. June 25
C. July 1
D. July 10

19. In an incident kept secret until quite recently, 749 American troops training for D-Day off Slapton Sands in England died in tragic circumstances, when:

A. They were shelled with live ammunition on the beach
B. Two of their LST's collided and quickly sank in deep water
C. An escorting medium bomber crashed into their ship, setting it afire
D. German E-boats torpedoed 3 LST's, sinking 2

20. The city of Caen, one of the early objectives of the invasion, proved a major obstacle to British and Canadian forces on the eastern edge of the battle front. The city finally fell on:

A. June 16
B. June 28
C. July 5
D. July 8

21. The "Falaise Pocket" was:

A. A surrounded group of German forces
B. An Allied salient cut off by a German counterattack
C. A haven for French Resistance forces south of the Allied lines
D. An unauthorized uniform alteration used by German occupying forces to stash loot in

22. The "bocage" was:

A. The famous cheese of the Southern region of Normandy, popular with both Germans and Allies
B. The name for the hedgerow countryside in Normandy
C. The nickname of the local Resistance forces
D. A French antitank rifle used by the Germans with little success

23. The farm country in Normandy was characterized by small rectangular fields bounded by dense hedgerows, or raised earthen walls topped by vegetation. These hedgerows provided the Nazis with strong, well-concealed defensive positions, which slowed down the Allied advance. The locally improvised Culin Hedgerow Device, named for its American sergeant inventor, was:

A. A gunsight and barrel attachment which permitted the user to shoot around corners, foiling ambushes
B. A powerful shaped explosive charge which blew large holes in hedgerows, permitting passage
C. A cutting fence, made of discarded German beach obstacles, which, welded on the front of tanks, allowed them to cut through hedgerows, rather than expose their undersides while climbing over
D. A high-pressure water hose which directed a stream of water onto the base of the hedgerow, washing it away so vehicles could pass through

24. As the landing area in Normandy had no natural harbors, the Allied planners devised a concrete artificial harbor designed to be towed across the English Channel and sunk in place off the beach. These Mulberry harbors:

A. Sank while being towed across the Channel and were lost
B. Did not fit in place as planned, and were abandoned
C. Were a success, but were severely damaged in storms a few weeks after D-Day
D. Worked so well that they are still in use today

25. Allied aircraft used in D-Day operations had conspicuous recognition markings consisting of:

A. Black and white stripes painted around fuselage and wings
B. Yellow cowlings, wing tips, and fuselage band
C. Solid white tail surfaces
D. Strings of amber lights on the wing leading edges

D-Day Answer Key

1. C	6. B	11. C	16. A	21. A
2. B	7. E	12. C	17. A	22. B
3. F	8. C	13. A	18. D, D	23. B
4. D	9. B	14. A	19. D	24. C
5. A	10. B	15. B	20. D	25. A

Army, Army Air Forces, and Navy
Slang

A "brass hat" is an officer of at least
one rank higher than you whom you
don't like and who doesn't like you.

Kenneth C. Royall

What do the following Army slang words signify?

1. ___ 5 x 5   A. A first sergeant
    (Five by five)   B. Medals and decorations
2. ___ Goldbrick   C. Intelligence section
3. ___ Fruit salad   D. A newly minted second lieutenant
4. ___ Topkick   E. A uniform stripe for years of service
5. ___ G-2   F. "I read you loud and clear"
6. ___ Shavetail   G. An easy, safe job, or one who seeks or obtains
7. ___ Hash mark   one

And these Navy terms?

8. ___ Pig boat   A. A Navy captain
9. ___ Tin can   B. One who has crossed the Equator
10. ___ Shellback   C. An aircraft carrier
11. ___ Four-striper   D. A destroyer
12. ___ Splinter Navy   E. A submarine
13. ___ Flattop   F. The Coast Guard Reserve

How about this Air Force terminology?

14. ___ Brolly   A. Abort a mission
15. ___ Scrub   B. Fighter escort aircraft
16. ___ Little Friend   C. Inflatable life vest
17. ___ Mae West   D. Low-level, strafing fighter sweep
18. ___ Rhubarb   E. Most dangerous position in bomber
19. ___ Coffin corner   formation
20. ___ Tail-end   F. Most dangerous position on a fighter mission
        Charlie   G. A parachute (from RAF usage)

And these Army vehicles?

21. ___ Peep   A. Late model Sherman tank with improved
22. ___ Deuce-and-a-   suspension, and more powerful 76mm. cannon
        half   B. 2½ ton amphibious truck
23. ___ Easy 8   C. Armored corps name for a jeep
24. ___ Duck   D. Popular, large 6-wheel Army truck

Army, Army Air Forces, and Navy Slang Answer Key

1. F	7. E	13. C	19. E
2. G	8. E	14. G	20. F
3. B	9. D	15. A	21. C
4. A	10. B	16. B	22. D
5. C	11. A	17. C	23. A
6. D	12. F	18. D	24. B

The Chow Line

An army marches on its stomach.

Napoleon Bonaparte

The U.S. Army developed a number of scientifically designed rations for field and combat troops, designating each with a letter or other symbol. Which ration was which:

1. ___ "C" ration
2. ___ "D" ration
3. ___ "K" ration
4. ___ "A" ration
5. ___ "B" ration
6. ___ "10-in-1" ration

A. Field ration using fresh milk, fruit, and vegetables
B. Variety package to supply a number of men in combat zone for one day
C. Field ration substituting canned milk, fruit, and vegetables for fresh where necessary
D. Balanced meal in cans for men cut off from normal food supply
E. Fortified chocolate bars for emergency use, discontinued after misuse
F. Compact, lightweight meals for combat and assault troops

For most servicemen, familiarity with military food bred contempt. Some of the slang terms reflect this dislike: (You must use one answer twice.)

7. ___ Armored cow
8. ___ Battery acid
9. ___ Collision mat (Navy usage)
10. ___ Dog food (or Kennel rations)
11. ___ Mud
12. ___ SOS

A. Coffee
B. Pancakes or waffles
C. Corned beef hash
D. Creamed chipped beef on toast
E. Canned condensed milk

13. The lemon drink mix in C-rations was:

A. The most popular beverage included
B. Often used successfully as hair rinse and floor cleaner
C. Discontinued early due to its unpopularity
D. B and C

14. The "K" ration was originally called the:

A. Iron ration
B. Armored ration
C. Paratrooper ration
D. Composition ration

15. The "10-in-1" ration evolved from the:

A. Jungle ration
B. Mountain ration
C. 5-in-1 ration
D. British "compo" or 14-in-1 ration
E. All of the above

16. The Air Forces Pocket Lunch, intended for use in single-seat fighter airplanes, consisted of:

A. An easy-opening can of fruit salad
B. A miniature sandwich on crackers
C. A mixture of confections
D. Fortified chocolate bars

17. The "Ration, Parachute, Emergency" weighed how much and contained how many calories?

A. 5 oz., 350 calories
B. 7½ oz., 500 calories
C. 11½ oz., 1,062 calories
D. 15 oz., 1,520 calories

The Chow Line Answer Key

1. D	7. E	13. D
2. E	8. A	14. C
3. F	9. B	15. E
4. A	10. C	16. C
5. C	11. A	17. C
6. B	12. D	

Landmines
A Potpourri of Questions to Blow Your Mind

Shoot first and inquire afterwards,
and if you make mistakes,
I will protect you.

Hermann Goering

Some of these questions do not fit neatly into any of the preceding categories; the answers to others would be self-evident if the questions were included in those chapters. Here goes!

1. On August 31, 1939, the Germans staged an incident which they used to provoke their attack on Poland. It consisted of:

A. A phony attack, supposedly by the Polish Army, on a Silesian border village in Germany
B. A bombing raid on an East Prussian town by the Luftwaffe posing as the Polish Air Force
C. Naval shelling of the city of Kolberg, purportedly by the Polish Navy
D. Artillery and mortar shelling of a Pomeranian town, by the Wehrmacht, but attributed to the Poles

2. When a top-secret radar set aboard a Luftwaffe night fighter plane wound up in Switzerland, the Swiss destroyed it in exchange for:

A. $5 million in gold
B. The sale of 12 Messerschmitt 109G aircraft
C. A German promise to end overflights by the Luftwaffe
D. 25 new Tiger tanks

3. The Belgian fort of Eben Emael fell to the Germans in May, 1940:

A. Under constant shelling by German 42cm howitzers
B. To 55 paratroopers who landed on the fortress roof in gliders
C. Due to sabotage by disloyal Belgian troopers in the fort's garrison
D. After costly frontal assaults by the Wehrmacht

4. General Sikorski, former Prime Minister of Poland, and commander of the Polish Army in exile, died:

A. By an assassin's bullet while reviewing Polish troops in North Africa
B. In the battle for Monte Cassino, while leading his troops there
C. When his airplane crashed into the Mediterranean upon takeoff from Gibraltar
D. In the final phase of the 1944 Warsaw Uprising

5. The Mannerheim Line was:

A. A telephone transmission line strung by front-line German communications troops in Poland in 1939
B. The official party propaganda line of the Free Germany Committee, the exiled German Communists in Moscow
C. The Finnish defense line against the Soviet attack in 1940
D. The Austrian steamship line, appropriated by the Nazis in 1939

6. The British or Commonwealth officer who destroyed the most Axis aircraft was:

A. S/Ldr George ("Buzz" or "Screwball") Beurling, RCAF
B. Lt. Col. "Paddy" Mayne, SAS
C. Grp/Capt. Peter Townsend, RAF
D. Grp/Capt. C.R. "Killer" Caldwell, RAAF

7. M3 was the U.S. Army designation for:

A. The "Grease Gun" .45 cal. submachine gun
B. The "Stuart" light tank
C. The "Grant-Lee" medium tank
D. A half-track armored personnel carrier
E. All of the above
F. A and C above only

Sherman and other Allied tank chassis were converted to self-propelled guns or armored personnel carriers. Match the following names to their vehicles:

8. ___ Sexton
9. ___ Priest
10. ___ Archer
11. ___ Kangaroo
12. ___ Bishop

A. 105mm. howitzer on Sherman chassis
B. A tank or SP vehicle with armament removed, used as personnel carrier
C. 25-pdr mounted on Valentine chassis
D. 25-pdr on Ram (Canadian Sherman) chassis
E. 17-pdr antitank gun on Valentine chassis

13. "Anzio Annie" was:

A. Mussolini's mistress in 1942
B. A German railway artillery piece which shelled the Anzio beachhead
C. The Italian propaganda counterpart to "Tokyo Rose" and "Axis Sally"
D. A popular dancer, prostitute, and spy in Italy, working for British intelligence in 1941

14. The Red Army news photographer Tyomin "scooped" his colleagues by taking the first photo of the Red flag over the Reichstag from an airplane. He then flew to Moscow in Marshal Zhukov's plane, and back to Berlin with the Red Army newspaper victory edition with his photo just as his fellow press members arrived. In his absence, Zhukov had:

A. Awarded him the Order of the Red Star
B. Ordered him shot for stealing the plane
C. Given Tyomin up for lost, along with the aircraft
D. Ordered the Red Army to withdraw from the Reichstag area under heavy fire

15. The nickname "Black Death" was bestowed by the Nazi forces on:

A. The Latvian Waffen SS division, which fought on to the very end in Berlin
B. The Royal Marine Commandos of the Royal Navy
C. The Soviet Black Sea Marines
D. U.S. Coast Guard antisubmarine forces

16. The Katyn forest, west of Smolensk in the USSR, is best known for:

A. Harboring large numbers of Soviet partisans, who fought off all Nazi attempts to eliminate them
B. A major German breakthrough in 1941, in which German Panzers emerged from the forest unexpectedly, scoring great success
C. The massacre in 1940 of over 4,000 Polish officers and men captured by the Russians in 1939
D. Being the center of a major German pincer movement, which cut off hundreds of thousands of Russians who were made prisoners

17. The Russian advance on Berlin was massive. The Soviet forces included:

A. 500,000 men and 2,100 tanks
B. 1 million men and 3,200 tanks
C. 2 million men and 6,300 tanks
D. 3½ million men and 8,000 tanks

18. The German 250th Division (Blue Division, or *Division Azul*) was made up of Spanish Fascist "volunteers." They fought near Leningrad from late 1941 to early 1944, but were disbanded when:

A. Casualties had become so high that the division practically ceased to exist as a functional unit
B. The division retreated in great disorder when beset by massed Russian troops and tanks in a major counterattack
C. Lack of equipment and language difficulties between Germans and Spaniards caused the division to fail in an important German thrust
D. England, protesting Spain's lack of neutrality, embargoed food and fuel shipments to Spain

19. An American division, whether fighting or not, was said to require _____ tons of supplies daily:

A. 175
B. 325
C. 650
D. 950

20. The neutral Swedes were in an awkward position during World War II. They traded with both the Germans and the Allies, with iron ore and steel products important among their exports. How much iron ore did Sweden export to Germany in 1943:

A. 1 million tons, 5% of German needs
B. 4 million tons, 20% of German needs
C. 6 million tons, 38% of German needs
D. 10 million tons, 28% of German needs

21. The Swedish government refused to supply German troops in Narvik, but did allow the Germans to:

A. Fly bombers over Sweden en route to Norway
B. Transport a total of 2 million German troops to and from Norway between July, 1940, and August 1943
C. Buy several thousand Bofors anti-aircraft guns
D. Use Swedish naval bases for supply and repairs until May, 1943

22. On October 1 and 2, 1943, the Nazis went to round up the Jews of Denmark for deportation and extermination. The Danish underground knew of these plans, and hid or smuggled out:

A. 2,000 of 3,500 Jews
B. 5,000 of 6,000 Jews
C. 7,500 of 8,000 Jews
D. 9,000 of 11,000 Jews

23. The U.S. Army Veterinary Service, a branch of the Medical Services, had several important missions. What is the correct order of their importance?

A. ___ Conduct veterinary laboratory services concerned with food and various types of research
B. ___ Inspect food for the military, including processing and sanitation of food processors
C. ___ Provide comprehensive animal service
D. ___ Coordinate reestablishment of veterinary services, livestock and production of biologicals in war-torn lands

24. Before U.S.-trained war dogs arrived in Europe after the Channel crossing in June, 1944, the Army and Army Air Forces obtained the dogs they used in Britain from:

A. The British Ministry of Aircraft Production
B. The Royal Army Medical Corps
C. The Humane Society of Great Britain
D. The Royal Navy Volunteer Reserve

Women served in the armed forces and auxiliary services of most major combatants. Identify the following from their acronyms:

25. ___ WAAC
26. ___ WAVES
27. ___ WASPS
28. ___ SPARS

A. Women pilots
B. Women in the U.S. Army
C. Women in the U.S. Navy
D. Women in the U.S. Coast Guard

Some of the British, Commonwealth and German women's services follow and also need to be matched up:

29. ___ ATA
30. ___ WAAS
    (Waasies)
31. ___ WRNS
    (Wrens)
32. ___ RAD

A. Labor service for German women
B. Women in the British Royal Navy
C. Women aircraft ferry pilots
D. South African women's services

33. Cold injury, such as frostbite and trench foot, is a debilitating condition suffered most often by infantry troops in cold, wet climates. The U.S. Army experienced many cases of trench foot, primarily in the winter of 1944-45. How many cases of cold injury were there in the Army in World War II, and how many of these were in early 1945?

A. 30,000 cases, 25,000 in 1945
B. 50,000 cases, 30,000 in 1945
C. 70,000 cases, 35,000 in 1945
D. 90,000 cases, 40,000 in 1945

34. Brazil declared war on Germany in 1942, and Brazilian air and naval forces participated in the battle against the U-Boats. What did the Brazilian army contribute to the war effort?

A. Brazilian troops trained for combat with the Americans, but only arrived in Europe at the end of hostilities
B. A Brazilian Expeditionary Force fought in Italy from the campaign near Naples to the end of the war
C. Brazilian forces furnished garrison troops in the Caribbean and West Africa
D. A Brazilian Expeditionary Force landed in Normandy, and fought all the way to Germany

American Lend-Lease shipments of military medical supplies went to many countries. The primary recipients, and amounts received were:

35. ___ Soviet Union   A. $50 million
36. ___ French Africa   B. $38 million
37. ___ United Kingdom and dominions   C. $5 million

38. In the winter of 1944, 23 dog sled teams were sent to France to help evacuate American wounded through the deep snow. These dogs:

A. Were a great success, but demand for them always exceeded supply
B. Were not used for their original purpose, as the snow melted as soon as the dogs arrived
C. Were eaten by the troops who were surrounded by Germans
D. Were eaten by French civilians in the area, who were cut off from their usual food supply

39. On October 14, 1943, 291 8th Air Force B-17's left England for Schweinfurt to bomb the ball-bearing factories there. How many B-17's did not return?

A. 25
B. 38
C. 50
D. 60

40. The Warsaw Uprising (by the Polish Home Army, months after the liquidation of the Warsaw Jewish ghetto) went on from:

A. July 1 to September 1, 1944
B. August 1 to October 9, 1944
C. September 2 to October 25, 1944
D. September 25 to October 9, 1944

41. The Soviet Army, which was only across the river from Warsaw, then took the city on:

A. September 24, 1944
B. October 27, 1944
C. December 23, 1944
D. January 17, 1945

Russian vocabulary quiz. What do these Russian words mean:

42. ___ Katyusha	A.	The muddy season
43. ___ Stavka	B.	Deliberate ramming of enemy aircraft with one's own fighter
44. ___ Taran		
45. ___ Shtormovik	C.	Red Army General Staff
46. ___ Rasputitsa	D.	An armored ground attack airplane
	E.	A bombardment rocket

47. The Soviet Army autopsy report on the body of Adolf Hitler stated that:

A. Hitler shot himself
B. Hitler poisoned, rather than shot, himself
C. Hitler had only one testicle
D. Someone tested the poison on Hitler's favorite dog, Blondi
E. A and C above
F. B, C, and D above

Landmine Answer Key

1. A	11. B	21. B	31. B	41. D
2. B	12. C	22. C	32. A	42. E
3. B	13. B	23. B, C, A, D	33. D	43. C
4. C	14. B	24. A	34. B	44. B
5. C	15. C	25. B	35. B	45. D
6. B	16. C	26. C	36. C	46. A
7. E	17. C	27. A	37. A	47. F
8. D	18. D	28. D	38. B	
9. A	19. C	29. C	39. D	
10. E	20. D	30. D	40. B	

FURTHER READING

There are too many books about World War II to list all of them here.

A number of excellent pictorial works exist. There are two useful series, each containing numerous color and black-and-white illustrations of aircraft, armored vehicles, uniforms and insignia: the Arco-Aircam series on individual aircraft and air forces; and the Osprey series (from Britain) entitled "Men-at-Arms" (for uniforms, etc.) and "Vanguard" (for armored vehicles and campaigns). Squadron/Signal publications issues a number of illustrated books about tanks and warplanes. The Profile series from England, long out of print, but now becoming available again, is a series of many small booklets covering armor and aircraft. Local bookstores or hobby shops may stock many of these.

Consult your local library about the U.S. government depository library nearest you for the many publications by the Department of Defense and its predecessor agencies. *The U.S. Army in World War II* is a series of volumes covering World War II in infinite detail.

Among the best histories and memoirs about World War II in Africa and Europe is Dwight Eisenhower's classic *Crusade in Europe* (New York: Doubleday, 1948), a top-level view of Allied strategy and operations from North Africa to D-Day. Field Marshal Bernard Law Montgomery's histories include 3 volumes, paramount among them *El Alamein to the River Sangro* (London: Hutchinson, 1948). A German view of several fronts is Fridolin von Senger and Etterlin's *Neither Fear Nor Hope* (New York: Dutton, 1964), by the Axis commander at Monte Cassino and elsewhere in Italy. The Eastern Front is well-covered by Paul Carell (Paul Karl Schmidt) in *Hitler Moves East, 1941-43* (Boston: Little, Brown, 1965) and *Scorched Earth* (Boston: Little, Brown, 1970). Schmidt has also written *Foxes of the Desert* (London: McDonald, 1960), a history of the *Africa Korps*. Readers interested in naval war against U-Boats and German surface raiders may read Walter Karig's *Battle Reports, Volume 2: The Atlantic War* (New York: Farrar & Rinehart, 1945). Anthony Verrier's *The Bomber Offensive* (New York: Macmillan, 1969) is a detailed history of the RAF and USAAF air actions against Germany.

WORLD WAR II
TRIVIA QUIZ BOOK

VOLUME II: THE PACIFIC

FORGOTTEN FACTS ABOUT
THIS CENTURY'S BIGGEST LAND GRAB

BY ERHARD KONERDING

MJF BOOKS
NEW YORK

CONTENTS

Answers are located at the end of each chapter.

The Japanese usually refer to World War II as the Pacific War, and most Americans will remember fighting on Pacific islands or in naval battles on that ocean. Yet the war against the Japanese also was fought in places like China, Thailand, Burma, the Netherlands East Indies, to the borders of India and Australia. The Japanese had been fighting China since the 1930's, and held much of that country until the final surrender.

"That great sea, miscalled the Pacific."

Charles Darwin, Journal . . .
During the Voyage . . . of
HMS *Beagle,* 1832-6

Pearl Harbor

War with America and Britain should still be avoidable when the overall situation is taken into consideration, and every effort should of course be made to that end.

Admiral Isoroku Yamamoto, after planning the Pearl Harbor attack in October, 1941.

The Japanese surprise attack on Pearl Harbor, Hawaii, on the quiet morning of December 7, 1941, plunged the United States into war, and practically overnight, united American public opinion in favor of war. War in Europe had been waged since September, 1939, and the Japanese and Chinese had been fighting since 1931!

1. In a security order of October 14, 1941, Admiral Husband Kimmel, Commander in Chief of the Pacific Fleet, warned that declaration of war by Japan might be preceded by:

A. A surprise attack on ships in Pearl Harbor
B. A surprise submarine attack on ships in the operating areas
C. A surprise attack on the Dutch naval base at Ambon
D. A and B only
E. A and C only

2. The signal for launching the Japanese aircraft was "Climb Mount Niitaka." Mount Niitaka, highest peak in the Japanese Empire, is in:

A. Hokkaido
B. Manchuria
C. Formosa (Taiwan)
D. Kyushu

3. The Japanese attack on Pearl Harbor and the surrounding installations took the lives of more than 2,300 Americans. How many Japanese aviators and aircraft were lost in the attack?

A. 10 aircraft, 25 aviators
B. 30 aircraft, 55 aviators
C. 50 aircraft, 78 aviators
D. 70 aircraft, 111 aviators

4. Although the Japanese sank or damaged a number of battleships and cruisers in the attack, they failed to destroy:

A. Any of the aircraft carriers, which were outside the harbor
B. The fuel oil stores in Hawaii
C. Repair facilities at Pearl Harbor
D. All of the above

5. Guns were lifted from several of the damaged battleships, repaired and reinstalled either in their former vessels or other battleships for use against the Axis. They were relined, repaired, and straightened where necessary, at Naval gun factories in:

A. San Diego, California
B. Pocatello, Idaho
C. Washington, D.C.
D. All of the above
E. B and C above

6. In November, 1941, in an action that convinced Japanese planners to attack Pearl Harbor and elsewhere, the United States demanded that the Japanese withdraw from:

A. Malaya
B. China
C. Indochina
D. Korea
E. B and C
F. C and D

7. U.S. Army Air Corps planes at Wheeler Field and elsewhere were parked practically wingtip-to-wingtip outside their hangars, which made them easy targets for the attacking Japanese. The aircraft were parked close together in order to:

A. Protect them from sabotage
B. Make them easier to service
C. Present a neater appearance during inspections by the Army commander in Hawaii

The two waves of attacking Japanese naval aircraft contained a mix of bombers and fighters. How many of each type altogether?

8. ___ Horizontal bombers   A. 40
9. ___ Dive bombers   B. 81
10. ___ Torpedo bombers   C. 104
11. ___ Zero fighters   D. 135

The Japanese claimed to have sunk four U.S. battleships, heavily damaged four others, and lightly damaged one. What was the actual fate of each of the battlewagons hit at Pearl?

12. ___ *Tennessee, Maryland,*   A. Sunk
     Pennsylvania   B. Sunk or beached, later salavaged
13. ___ *Nevada, California,*   C. Damaged
     West Virginia
14. ___ *Arizona, Oklahoma,*
     Utah, (former battleship
     used as target ship)

15. How many U.S. airplanes (Navy and Army) were destroyed in the Pearl Harbor attack:

A. 42
B. 96
C. 188
D. 352

16. Soldiers, sailors, and airmen performed many acts of extreme bravery and heroism during and after the surprise attack. Sixty Navy Crosses, sixty-five Silver Stars and five distinguished Service Crosses were awarded for that day. How many Medals of Honor (all to Navy men)?

A. 5
B. 10
C. 15
D. 20

17. Many men were rescued from the sunken battleships, often by crews cutting through the bottoms of the capsized hulls. Many more bodies were recovered during salvage operations. In a grisly discovery, salvagers found three bodies of men who, trapped in a storage room aboard the *West Virginia*, had apparently survived until:

A. December 10, 1941
B. December 15, 1941
C. December 23, 1941
D. December 31, 1941

Pearl Harbor Answer Key

1. D	7. A	13. B
2. C	8. C	14. A
3. B	9. D	15. C
4. D	10. A	16. C
5. E	11. B	17. C
6. E	12. C	

Geography

"If yer son Packy was to ask ye where the Ph'lippeens is, cud ye give him anny good idea whether they was in Rooshia or jus' west iv the tracks?

. . . "tis not more thin two months since ye larned whether they were islands or canned goods."

"On the Philippines"
in Mr. Dooley in Peace and War
by Finley Peter Dunne, 1898

While many Americans knew something of European geography, and were familiar with the names of many of the battle sites there, few Americans had ever heard of the remote Pacific islands where much of the fighting took place. British and Commonwealth residents were more likely to have an idea where places like Burma and Hong Kong were, though the names of villages and mountain ranges were probably unknown to them, also.

1. In November, 1938, the Japanese announced their "New Order in East Asia" which would comprise Japan and its "colonies." These colonies included:

A. Korea and Taiwan (Formosa)
B. The Micronesian mandate (granted Japan by the League of Nations)
C. Manchukuo (Manchuria), "reformed" China, i.e., without Chiang Kai-shek, and the Kwantung territory
D. South Sakhalin Island
E. All of the above
F. A and B above
G. B, C, and D above

2. The "Greater East Asia Co-Prosperity Sphere" was the intended expansion of the Japanese "New Order" to include more territory, especially the former European colonies and American possessions. This plan was announced:

A. October 1, 1939
B. January 1, 1940
C. August 1, 1940
D. August 11, 1941

3. Honolulu is approximately equidistant from all of the following pairs of places *except:*

A. Alaska and Samoa
B. Panama and the Philippines
C. Australia and Cape Horn
D. California and the Siberian shore

4. The island of Midway was named for its location, halfway between:

A. New Guinea and Australia
B. Manila and San Francisco
C. Tokyo and San Francisco
D. Tokyo and Honolulu

5. Many of the Japanese-held island groups in the Pacific were former German colonies mandated to Japan by the League of Nations. Which island or islands were *not* among those mandated?

A. Palau
B. Saipan and Tinian
C. Kwajalein
D. Guadalcanal

Can you place each island within its island group?

6. ___ Saipan	A. Volcano Islands
7. ___ Kwajalein	B. The Marianas
8. ___ Iwo Jima	C. The Marshalls
9. ___ Truk	D. The Solomons
10. ___ Guadalcanal	E. The Carolines

Many of the Pacific islands were in the Tropics. Which were North of the Equator, and which South?

11. ___ North	A. Solomons
12. ___ South	B. Peleliu
	C. Truk
	D. Marianas

13. In 1942, the boundary between the South Pacific Area, under Admiral Nimitz, and the Southwest Pacific Area, under General MacArthur, was shifted from 160° West Longitude to 159°. This was done so that:

A. The number of square miles in each command would be exactly the same
B. Marines could fight on Guadalcanal
C. Port Moresby, Papua, would be included in MacArthur's command
D. More land would be in the Southwest Pacific Area

14. The Japanese timetable for the initial attacks in the Pacific included air strikes and landings in several areas. Can you put the planned operations in correct order?

A. Air attacks on Pearl Harbor and Oahu
B. Initial assault on Hong Kong
C. Landings in Siam
D. Landings in Malaya
E. First air attacks on Luzon

15. Canadian soldiers played a major part in the European campaigns in World War II. What part did they play in the Pacific campaigns?

A. Canadian officers and men were assigned to posts in Australian units fighting on Pacific islands
B. Canadian units joined in the unsuccessful defense of Hong Kong until its fall to the Japanese in December, 1941
C. They participated in the campaigns on Attu and Kiska in the Aleutian Islands
D. The Canadian government offered to send men to help in the invasion of the Japanese home islands
E. All of the above
F. A and C above

16. All North American nations sent military units to the Pacific. The Mexican government, in fact, sent its first unit ever to serve outside Mexico. It was:

A. The frigate *Santa Ana,* which bombarded Okinawa during the American landings there, and defended the fleet against Kamikaze attacks
B. The 201st Mexican fighter squadron *(Escadrilla Aguilas Aztecas)* which flew support missions in the Philippines in 1945
C. The 401st Infantry Regiment *(Las Incas),* who distinguished themselves in the recapture of Manila in 1945
D. The 33rd Armored Squadron *(Los Caballeros de Oaxaca),* whose Sherman tanks supported American infantry on Okinawa

17. Japanese midget submarines were spotted, sunk, and captured at Pearl Harbor. They were also used at:

A. Sydney Harbor, Australia
B. Madagascar
C. Calcutta, India
D. A and B above
E. A and C above

18. Korea was a Japanese colony long before war broke out. Koreans served in the Japanese war effort, willingly or unwillingly, as:

A. Laborers
B. Soldiers
C. Sailors
D. Prostitutes ("Comfort girls", or *Chosenpi*)
E. All of the above
F. A and D only

American GI's and Marines, British and Australian fighting men often renamed local geographic features in their battle areas. Where are these located?

19. ___ Ironbottom Sound   A. New Guinea
20. ___ The Golden Stairs   B. Okinawa
      (dubbed by Australians)   C. Saipan
21. ___ Sugar Loaf   D. Biak
22. ___ Purple Heart Ridge   E. Guadalcanal
23. ___ The Sump

Other sites remained known by their local names, or those given by the imperial powers who had ruled the areas. (Use one geographical name twice).

24. ___ Mt. Tapotchau   A. Leyte, Philippines
25. ___ Noemfoor Island (near which place)   B. Okinawa
26. ___ Ormoc Valley   C. India
27. ___ Kokoda Trail   D. Guam
28. ___ Shuri Castle   E. New Guinea
29. ___ Kohima

30. Negro (black) members of the 24th Infantry and the 93rd Division of the 25th Infantry fought mainly on:
A. Okinawa
B. Luzon, Philippines
C. Bougainville
D. Guadalcanal

The U.S. Army Air Forces numbered the various air forces, according to geographical areas of service. Where were each of these based: (use one geographical name twice)

31. ___ 5th AF	A.	China
32. ___ 7th AF	B.	Southwest Pacific (Solomons to Philippines)
33. ___ 10th AF	C.	India, Burma, China
34. ___ 11th AF	D.	Aleutians (bombed Japan)
35. ___ 13th AF	E.	Central and Western Pacific
36. ___ 14th AF	F.	India (bombed Japan, Formosa, Thailand,
37. ___ 20th AF		Burma)

38. "Broadway" and "Piccadilly" were code names in early 1944 for:

A. USS *Chattanooga* and HMS *Hereford*
B. Two landing areas in Burma
C. Admiral Mountbatten and General Stilwell
D. Manila and Singapore

39. On June 3, 1942, Japanese aircraft from the carrier *Ryujo* bombed targets in a diversion intended to distract American forces from the planned Midway attack. They hit:

A. Guadalcanal, Solomon Islands
B. Dutch Harbor and Unalaska, Alaska
C. Lahaina, Hawaii

40. One of the farthest-ranging Japanese air raids, on April 5, 1942, hit:

A. Calcutta, India
B. Port Darwin, Australia
C. Colombo, Ceylon
D. Delhi, India

41. The Soviet Union declared war on Japan late in the war. The Russians and Japanese had already fought, at places like Nomonhan and Khalkin-Gol on the Manchurian border, in:

A. Spring, 1937
B. Autumn, 1939
C. Summer, 1940
D. Winter, 1940-41

42. The first Allied force to enter Rangoon, Burma, at Mingaladon, was:

A. An RAF bomber crew in their Mosquito aircraft
B. An Indian Army tank crew in a Grant tank
C. A "stick" of Gurkha paratroopers
D. Royal Marine commandos who paddled their rubber boat up the Irrawaddy River

43. The Eighth Route Army was a force of:

A. American OSS agents in Indochina
B. Communist Chinese forces opposing the Japanese
C. Nationalist Chinese forces
D. British and Indian troops in Malaya

44. The Japanese occupied French Indochina in 1940, soon after the fall of France to the Nazis. The Japanese army took over complete control, after attacking French military posts, on:

A. October 11, 1940
B. January 23, 1942
C. December 1, 1943
D. March 9, 1945

After the surrender of Japan, Indochina and Korea were occupied by Allied forces who were to supervise the surrender of Japanese forces there. Both lands were divided arbitrarily. These temporary divisions became borders; the one in Korea is practically the same today. Who occupied what?

45. ___ Indochina above 16 North Latitude	A.	Soviets
46. ___ Indochina below 16 North Latitude	B.	British
47. ___ Korea above 38 North Latitude	C.	Americans
48. ___ Korea below 38 North Latitude	D.	Nationalist Chinese

49. *The Bridge on the River Kwai,* a novel by Pierre Boulle, also author of *Planet of the Apes*, was fiction, though based on a true incident. After the bridge in Thailand was completed, the healthy surviving Allied prisoners, mostly Australians and British, were shipped to Japan to work there. Enroute, their ships sank,

A. Gunned down in error by Japanese cruisers and destroyers
B. Torpedoed by two American submarines
C. Some of the survivors were picked up by Japanese vessels, then sent to work in Japan
D. Some of the survivors were picked up by U.S submarines
E. A and C above
F. B, C and D above

50. The Australian Army in 1945, performed major landings in the area of:

A. Malaya and Singapore
B. Brunei
C. Dutch Borneo
D. Thailand
E. B and C above

Geography Answer Key

1. E	11. B, C, D	21. B	31. B	41. B
2. C	12. A	22. C	32. E	42. A
3. C	13. B	23. D	33. C	43. B
4. C	14. D,A,C,E,B	24. D	34. D	44. D
5. D	15. E	25. E	35. B	45. D
6. B	16. B	26. A	36. A	46. B
7. C	17. D	27. E	37. F	47. A
8. A	18. E	28. B	38. B	48. C
9. E	19. E	29. C	39. B	49. F
10. D	20. A	30. C	40. C	50. E

People

What kind of people do they
(the Japanese) think we are?

Winston Churchill

About famous, infamous, and unknown participants in the Pacific War.

Two Japanese admirals had similar American connections. Both Admiral
Isoroku Yamamoto, the planner of the Pearl Harbor attack, and Vice
Admiral Seiichi Ito, who went down with the mighty battleship *Yamato,*
had studied in the U.S. and spent other time there. Match each admiral
with his American experiences:

1. ___ Yamamoto   A. Naval attache in Washington in the 1920's
2. ___ Ito   B. Studied at Harvard University
                      C. Graduate of Yale University
                      D. Friend in the 1920's of future Admiral
                         Spruance, then assistant of U.S. Naval
                         Intelligence
                      E. Learned poker and crap games while in U.S.

3. Charles Lindbergh, famous flyer, had resigned his AAF commission in a
dispute with FDR. He later:

A. Shot down a Japanese plane, and was nearly shot down himself, while
   flying P-38's in the Pacific
B. Flew F4U Corsairs in the Pacific
C. Helped Ford Motor Co. to build B-24's at the Willow Run factory.
D. Regained his commission by special order of FDR in honor of his
   service to the U.S.
E. All of the above
F. A, B, and C only

4. World War I flying ace Captain Eddie Rickenbacker made headlines when he and others aboard a ditched B-17 were rescued after 24 days aboard a rubber raft off Hawaii. At that time he was:

A. President of Eastern Airlines
B. A pilot for Air Transport Command
C. Carrying a secret message for General MacArthur
D. Demonstrating the B-17's capabilities to the U.S. Navy when the plane went out of control
E. A and C above
F. All of the above

5. Ernie Pyle, the beloved war correspondent and author of *G.I. Joe*, was killed by Japanese machine-gun fire on:

A. Kerama Retto
B. Ie Shima
C. Okinawa
D. Iwo Jima

6. USMC Major Gregory "Pappy" Boyington, skipper of the "Black Sheep" squadron:

A. Received the Medal of Honor for his actions in the Solomons
B. Was also a "Flying Tiger" pilot
C. Returned to the States for a triumphant War Bond tour in 1945
D. Spent a year in Japanese captivity after his plane went down
E. A, B, and C above
F. A, B, and D above

7. Japan's leading flying ace at the end of the war was:

A. Kazuo Sakamaki
B. Saburo Sakai
C. Toshiro Mifune
D. Miyamoto Musashi

8. General Douglas MacArthur was rarely seen without his distinctive peaked cap. It was:

A. The cap he wore as an acting Brigadier General in World War I
B. His Field Marshal's cap, which he first wore in the Philippines in 1936
C. A USAAF Major General's cap
D. Kept on a hat stretcher at night after it shrank aboard the PT boat while departing Philippines
E. A and D above
F. B and D above

Several American authors wrote of their experiences in World War II. Who served where?

9. ___ Norman Mailer
   (The Naked and the Dead)
10. ___ James Jones
    (From Here to Eternity, The Thin Red Line)
11. ___ William Manchester
    (MacArthur: American Caesar, Goodbye Darkness)

A. Marine enlisted man on Okinawa
B. Army enlisted man, fought in Philippines
C. Army enlisted man, served from before Pearl Harbor to Guadalcanal campaign

The late President John F. Kennedy was famous as skipper of the PT-109 in the South Pacific. Other political personalities, both living and dead, also served in that theater. Can you match them?

12. ___ Barry Goldwater (Senator from Arizona)
13. ___ George Bush (Vice President)
14. ___ Joseph McCarthy (late Senator from Minnesota)
15. ___ Gerald Ford (former President)
16. ___ John Glenn (Ohio Senator)
17. ___ Lyndon Johnson (late President)
18. ___ Richard Nixon (former President)

A. USN gunnery officer, served aboard CVL USS *Monterey*
B. USMC pilot in the Pacific, ace
C. Youngest Navy pilot, won DFC and Navy Crosses, shot down in Pacific, and rescued by U.S. submarine!
D. Navy officer, awarded Silver Star for B-26 mission
E. South Pacific Combat Air Transport ground officer in U.S. Navy
F. USMC administrative officer, was "tail gunner" on some operational flights, "wounded" during Equator crossing ceremony!
G. USAAF Air Transport Command pilot, flew "hump" missions

19. In 1949, Iva Ikuko Toguri D'Aquino was convicted in a Federal court in California of treason. She had been denounced as the "one and only Tokyo Rose." She:

A. Never called herself Tokyo Rose on the radio, only spoke on the air 2 to 3 minutes a day, mostly in 1943 and 1944
B. Gave up her American citizenship for that of Japan
C. Helped the Allied POW's who wrote her scripts
D. Was trapped in Japan in 1941 without a U.S. passport, but always considered herself a loyal American
E. A and B above
F. A, B, and C above
G. A, C, and D above

20. U.S. Navy Ensign George Gay, was:

A. The dive bomber pilot who was credited with sinking the Japanese battleship *Yamato*
B. The only survivor of Torpedo Squadron Eight in the Battle of Midway, who saw the whole battle after ditching
C. The first Navy officer to receive the Medal of Honor, for rescuing sailors aboard the doomed USS *Arizona*
D. Captain of PT-41, the boat on which General MacArthur left Luzon

The Japanese generals and admirals who commanded the forces on islands attacked by the U.S. Army and Marines all died on those islands, most by suicide when the situation was hopeless. Who commanded which island?

21. ___ Iwo Jima
22. ___ Okinawa
23. ___ Saipan
24. ___ Guam
25. ___ Tarawa
26. ___ Peleliu

A. Lt. Gen. Yoshitsugu Saito and V. Adm. Chuichi Nagumo (Pearl Harbor hero, disgraced after Midway defeat)
B. R. Adm. Keiji Shibasaki
C. Lt. Gen. Tadamichi Kuribayashi
D. Lt. Gen. Mitsuru Ushijima
E. Col. Kunio Nakagawa (island group commanded by Lt. Gen. Sadae Inoue)
F. Lt. Gen. Takashi Takashima

27. The top U.S. Army ace in the Pacific was Major Richard "Bing" Bong, with 40 kills. He later:

A. Was elected governor of South Dakota
B. Was captured by the Japanese after bailing out over Mindanao and executed
C. Died testing the experimental P-80 jet fighter
D. Became the first general to command fighter forces for the newly-created U.S. Air Force in 1947

28. Ensign Kazuo Sakamaki became the first Japanese prisoner taken by U.S. forces, after he:

A. Crash-landed his crippled Zero fighter at Kaneohe Naval Air Station after strafing the field on December 7, 1941
B. Ran his midget submarine aground on Oahu during the Pearl Harbor attack
C. Fell overboard from his destroyer off Manila and was picked up by a PT boat
D. Bailed out of his damaged torpedo bomber and landed near the blazing USS *Shaw*

29. General Holland M. Smith, USMC, commander of the landing force on Tarawa, and assault commander on Saipan, was known by the nickname:

A. Hell and High Water
B. Hurt 'em Mightily
C. Howlin' Mad
D. Hooligan Mike

30. General Tomoyuki Yamashita, known as the "Tiger of Malaya" for his conquest of that British colony:

A. Committed suicide in Tokyo upon hearing of Japan's surrender
B. Was captured by the British in Burma, and sentenced to life in prison for ordering British fliers executed
C. Was hanged by U.S. authorities for atrocities committed by his troops in the Philippines
D. Became director of the resurrected Mitsubishi company in 1948, and died the wealthiest man in Japan in 1972

31. Col. Philip Cochran, leader of the Air Commandos in Burma, was the model for "Flip Corkin" in the comic strip:

A. "Steve Canyon" by Milton Caniff
B. "Terry and the Pirates" by Milton Caniff
C. "Smilin' Jack" by Zack Mosley
D. "Buz Sawyer" by Roy Crane

Three marine officers who later became Commandants of the U.S Marine Corps received the Medal of Honor for action in the Pacific. Match with the time and place where he performed the deeds for which he won the medal: (note: one of these officers did *not* receive the Medal of Honor)

32. ___ Major General Alexander Vandegrift   A. Guam, 1944

33. ___ Colonel David Shoup   B. Solomon Islands, 1942

34. ___ Capt. Louis Wilson   C. Betio Island (Tarawa, Gilbert Islands), 1943

35. ___ Lt. Col. Lemuel C. Shepherd   D. Did not receive the Medal of Honor

36. More than 70 Marines, and nearly 90 Army soldiers won the Medal of Honor in the Pacific, many of them posthumously. How many were awarded the medal for sacrificing their lives for those of their comrades by falling onto exploding grenades?

A. 12   C. 23
B. 19   D. 31

37. Signalman Douglas Munro received the only Medal of Honor awarded a member of the U.S. Coast Guard in World War II. He was killed while protecting Marines evacuating from a surrounded beach. This was on:

A. Guadalcanal
B. Tarawa
C. Saipan
D. Okinawa

38. Black Americans engaged in the war in the Pacific in many capacities. Which was *not* among them?

A. Army combat troops
B. Marine combat troops
C. Navy stewards (and gun crew)
D. Army Air Force pilots
E. Navy Seabees

Many Major League baseball players joined the armed forces during the war, and a number served in combat. Which members of the Brooklyn and New York teams served in the Pacific?

39. ___ Ted Williams   A. Taught physical training to AAF cadets on
40. ___ Phil Rizzuto   mainland and Hawaii
41. ___ Joe DiMaggio   B. U.S. Marine antiaircraft gunner at Pearl
42. ___ Pee Wee Reese   Harbor, Tinian, Okinawa
43. ___ Gil Hodges   C. Marine Corps pilot
                         D. Caught malaria in New Guinea, then played
                            ball for Navy league team
                         E. U.S. Navy, rose to rank of CPO

44. Saburo Sakai, Japanese enlisted man and fighter pilot, attacked 8 TBF Grumman Avengers, thinking they were Wildcats, and was badly shot up by the torpedo planes' defensive guns. He:

A. Lost his right eye, and was temporarily partly paralyzed
B. Crashed and was taken prisoner by a PT boat crew
C. Flew back to his base at Rabaul, and landed safely
D. Shot down all of the American planes despite his wounds
E. A and C
F. B and D

45. Jimmy Doolittle, who led the daring 1942 raid on Tokyo, and later was promoted to Major General:

A. Had been a racing car driver at Indianapolis in the 1920's
B. Had been a prize-winning racing pilot for the Army
C. Had a Doctor of Science degree from M.I.T., and had taught there
D. All of the above
E. A and B above
F. B and C above

46. General "Vinegar Joe" Stilwell, American commander in China, disliked Generalissimo Chiang Kai-shek, and referred to him by the nickname:

A. "Chimp"
B. "Twerp"
C. "Peanut"
D. "Puppy Dog"

47. The last Japanese soldier to surrender was Lt. Hiroo Onoda, who was finally convinced that the war was over by his former commander. He gave up:

A. On Guam in 1965
B. On Borneo in 1968
C. In Malaya in 1970
D. In the Philippines in 1974

48. Gerhard Neuman, later to become chief of the jet engine division of General Electric corporation, lost his German citizenship by refusing to return to the *Reich* from China. He later:

A. Joined the "Flying Tigers" as a ground officer
B. Worked for the OSS in China
C. Was called "Herman the German"
D. All of the above
E. B and C above only

Netherlands Ministry of Defense (Navy)

49. Admiral K. Doorman (above), commander of Allied naval forces in The Battle of the Java Sea on February 27, 1942, was which nationality?

A. American
B. Australian
C. British
D. Dutch

50. The photo of the flag-raising over Iwo Jima became probably the best-known picture of the war. Of the five U.S. Marines and one Navy Corpsman who raised the flag over Mount Suribachi, how many came off the island alive?

A. Two
B. Three
C. Four
D. Five
E. None

51. Subhas Chandra Bose was:

A. The Major General commanding the Indian Army in Burma
B. Leader of the renegade Indian National Army which fought against the British, though many "deserted" to the British at the first opportunity
C. An Indian Army Subedar who won the Victoria Cross for bravery during the recapture of Rangoon, Burma
D. Commanding officer of HMIS *Vishnu,* the Indian Navy cruiser which went down with all hands off Akyab, Burma, in January, 1945. The captain went down with the ship

52. General Douglas MacArthur said, soon after leaving the Philippines and arriving in Australia: "I shall return." Who coined the expression originally?

A. Carlos Romulo, Philippine journalist
B. Manuel Quezon, President of the Philippines
C. An unnamed U.S. Army colonel of the Army Special Services

53. The officer pictured here in Burma or India, is:

A. Col. (later Brigadier) Orde Wingate, leader of the "Chindits"
B. Col. Philip Cochran, leader of the "Air Commandos"
C. Gen. Claire Lee Chennault of the "Flying Tigers"
D. Col. Frank D. Merrill, of "Merrill's Marauders"

54. In a characteristic pose, sitting atop a jeep to be better seen by the men under his command, in this case, American troops somewhere in the Southeast Asia command, is:

A. General "Vinegar Joe" Stilwell
B. Admiral Lord Louis Mountbatten
C. Generalissimo Chiang Kai-shek
D. General George Kenney

People Answer Key

1. A, B, E	12. G	23. A	34. A	45. F
2. A, C, D	13. C	24. F	35. D	46. C
3. F	14. F	25. B	36. D	47. D
4. E	15. A	26. E	37. A	48. D
5. B	16. B	27. C	38. D	49. D
6. F	17. D	28. B	39. C	50. B
7. B	18. E	29. C	40. E	51. B
8. F	19. G	30. C	41. A	52. A
9. B	20. B	31. B	42. D	53. A
10. C	21. C	32. B	43. B	54. B
11. A	22. D	33. C	44. E	

Naval Power

Gentlemen, you can do as you like with your ships but for two hundred years the people of the Indies have paid taxes to support a navy to defend their homes and that we are going to do. We may not win, but we shall go down defending the homes of the people of this country.

Vice Admiral C.E.L. Helfrich,
Royal Netherlands Navy, to
British and American military
contemplating withdrawal
before The Battle of the Java Sea

Ships of all sizes and all types fought in the Pacific War, and transports made the movement of enormous numbers of men and quantities of war-making material possible. The aircraft carrier in World War II in the Pacific proved itself as a major weapons system, able to project the awesome power of aircraft over vast distances. The aircraft carrier was perfectly suited to war in the Pacific, and influenced the conflict from Pearl Harbor to final attacks on the Japanese home islands.

A number of U.S. Navy submarine captains received the Congressional Medal of Honor. Two captains, however, gave up their lives in very different ways. One went down with the ship so the Japanese could capture neither him with his secret knowledge, nor the code books aboard the sub; the badly wounded skipper of another ordered "Take her down!" while he was still on the bridge after a collision with a Japanese gunboat.

1. ___ Cmdr. H.W. Gilmore,
   USS *Growler*
2. ___ Capt. John Cromwell,
   USS *Sculpin*

A. Went down with the ship off Truk, November 19, 1943
B. Ordered "Take her down!" in Southwest Pacific, February 7, 1943

3. During the battle of Leyte Gulf, Admiral Nimitz sent a message to Admiral Halsey, "Where is Repeat Where is Task Force Thirty Four RR The World Wonders." The last three words of the message were:

A. An error in the transcription
B. Padding by the communications officer who meant to distract Japanese cryptographers
C. A scathing criticism of Halsey's inaction
D. Added to the message after Japanese interception

In the Leyte Gulf battle, the Japanese lost many ships and practically ceased to exist as an effective navy. How many of each type were lost?

4. ___ Carriers	A. Three
5. ___ Battleships	B. Four
6. ___ Cruisers	C. Nine
7. ___ Destroyers	D. Ten

8. Of these participants, the only Allied survivors of The Battle of the Java Sea on February 27, 1942 were: (Soon after, the Japanese sank these survivors in the Sunda Strait!)

A. HNMS *Java* (Dutch cruiser)
B. USS *Houston* (American cruiser)
C. HMAS *Perth* (Australian cruiser)
D. HMS *Jupiter* (British destroyer)
E. B and C above
F. A and D above

9. The Japanese "Long Lance" torpedo, a great success in the early war years, was:

A. Fueled by oxygen
B. Faster than American or British torpedoes
C. Larger and with a more powerful warhead than American or British torpedoes
D. All of the above
E. A and C above only

10. The Navy V-12 program, for training and commissioning officers who were not already college graduates, was called V-12 since:

A. It was 12 months long
B. It was 12 semesters long
C. It was the twelfth officer training program
D. The admiral who originated the program decided to name it for the V-12 diesel engine used on motor launches

11. Six U.S. submarines sank nearly, or more than 100,000 tons of Japanese shipping (both merchant and war ships), or more than 20 Japanese vessels. Which were *not* among them?

A. *Barb* and *Tang*
B. *Flasher* and *Rasher*
C. *Silversides* and *Tautog*
D. *Shad* and *Chub*

12. This sailor is cleaning out:

A. The breech of a 16-inch naval gun
B. A torpedo tube
C. The reflector portion of a searchlight
D. The nose of a barrage balloon

13. The destroyer USS *Ward* fired the first American shots at Pearl Harbor, sinking a Japanese midget submarine in the wee hours of December 7. Three years later, to the day, the *Ward*, now a fast destroyer transport:

A. Was sunk by a Japanese midget submarine
B. Was damaged beyond repair by Kamikazes
C. Was ultimately sunk by fire from USS *O'Brien*, whose captain had skippered the *Ward* in 1941!
D. B and C above

14. The *Montana*-class battleships *Ohio, Maine, New Hampshire*, and *Louisiana* were never completed. They would have:

A. Carried twelve 16-inch guns in 4 turrets
B. Been essentially enlarged *Iowa*-class ships
C. Been even larger than the *Yamato* and *Musashi*
D. All of the above
E. A and B only

15. The German surface raider *Kormoran* sank HMAS *Sydney* in the Indian Ocean in November, 1942. The *Kormoran* later:

A. Returned to Germany through the British blockade, but never went to sea again
B. Sailed to Japan, and was taken over as a Japanese fast transport
C. Sank in the Indian Ocean, and her survivors sailed to Australia
D. Fled to the neutral Portuguese state of Goa on the Indian coast, and was interned for the rest of the war

16. The Japanese battleship *Yamato* was the largest warship ever built. It was sunk off Saipan by:

A. The USS *New Jersey* and USS *California*
B. The submarine USS *Croaker*
C. Land-based B-24 bombers
D. Carrier-based torpedo and bomber aircraft

17. Liberty ships, which carried cargo to U.S. and Allied forces worldwide, had several advantages over more traditionally constructed vessels. Liberty ships had arc-welded hulls, rather than riveted. This saved:

A. 13% in weight (since hull plates did not overlap, and the weight of welds was less than rivets)
B. 1/3 of the time usually spent in construction
C. 1/2 million rivets
D. All of the above

18. The "Higgins Boat," named for a New Orleans boat yard, was:

A. The standard motor launch aboard cruisers and battleships
B. The LCVP landing craft
C. A small rubber boat used by underwater demolition teams
D. A class of converted yachts used for patrolling

19. The USS *Langley,* once the collier *Jupiter,* was the first ship to serve as an aircraft carrier. In World War II, the *Langley:*

A. Served as an escort carrier until sunk by Japanese submarines in the Battle of the Coral Sea
B. Served as a seaplane tender, and was sunk by Japanese aircraft off Java while ferrying Army planes there in early 1942
C. Served as a fast transport until it was sunk by Japanese torpedo boats off Guadalcanal in mid-1942
D. Served as an oiler, and was destroyed in a collision with the USS *Forrest Sherman* in early 1943

20. The majority of Japanese merchant vessels were destroyed by United States:

A. Surface vessels
B. Land-based bombers
C. Carrier-based aviation
D. Submarines

21. A World War II American cruiser carried a coat of paint estimated to weigh:

A. 10 tons   C. 100 tons
B. 50 tons   D. 600 tons

22. U.S. Navy enlisted men's blue uniforms had a black neckerchief and a collar with three collar braids. They represent:

A. Admiral Farragut, and the War of 1812, Civil War, and Spanish-American War
B. Admiral Oliver Hazard Perry and his three major victories in the War of 1812
C. John Paul Jones, and the Revolutionary War, War of 1812, and Civil War
D. Lord Nelson, and the Battles of the Baltic, Nile, and Trafalgar

U.S. Navy officers' dress uniforms were blue or white, depending upon the season or the climate. Their working uniforms were:

23. ___ Summer working   A. Tan
24. ___ Winter working (later for dirty jobs)   B. Gray
25. ___ Aviation working   C. Medium blue
                                    D. Green

Both United States Navy and British Royal Navy flag officers' dress blue uniforms had stripes of braid on the trouser legs. They were referred to as:

26. ___ U.S. Navy   A. Lightning conductor pants
27. ___ Royal Navy   B. Snot-wiper pants
                      C. Railroad pants

28. In the Navy, a First Lieutenant is:

A. The rank between Second Lieutenant and Captain
B. A newly graduated Naval Academy cadet
C. The officer in charge of deck seamanship
D. The Lieutenant with the highest seniority aboard ship

29. Sometime in 1943, the U.S. Navy changed the colors of some features on its navigation charts, such as:

Land: Buff to gray

Navigation lights: orange to magenta

(Deep water and shoals were kept blue and green, respectively, though)

These color changes were:

A. Due to a shortage of the correct color inks
B. To conform with Army charts
C. So the charts would be easier to read at night
D. To make the charts more water-resistant

— U.S. National Archives

30. This vessel, shown bombarding a Japanese island with rockets, is an:

A. LST (R)
B. LSM (R)
C. LSD (R)
D. LCVP (R)

31. The British Royal Navy felt its aircraft carriers were superior to those of the U.S. Navy, since their carriers had:

A. Steam catapults for launching aircraft
B. Armored flight decks (rather than wooden) which better withstood battle damage
C. Turbine engines which made them faster than other ships
D. Been built on warship hulls, instead of merchant ship bottoms

32. The *Shinano* was a huge Japanese carrier. Which of the statements below are true?

A. It was laid down and partially built as a *Yamato*-class battleship, but finished as a carrier
B. *Shinano* was sunk by USS *Archerfish* on November 28, 1944, the largest warship ever sunk by a submarine
C. The ship was carrying 50 *Ohka* suicide rocket craft, which went to the bottom with it
D. *Shinano* had about the same dimensions as a U.S. *Essex*-class carrier, but about twice the displacement (weight of water displaced by the hull)
E. All of the above

33. The idea of aircraft carriers and gunships operating together, as a "Task Force," with the latter screening for the former, was originated by Admiral Reeves:

A. Of the U.S. Navy, in the early 1920's
B. Of the U.S. Navy, in the 1930's
C. Of the British Royal Navy, in the early 1920's
D. Of the British Royal Navy, in the 1930's

34. The escort carrier was an expedient, smaller aircraft carrier, usually built on a merchant ship hull. Airplanes from these small carriers regularly flew:

A. Air cover against enemy aircraft
B. Close air support
C. Anti-submarine patrol
D. All of the above
E. A and B only
F. B and C only

35. A fast carrier could make way at a full speed of:

A. 11 to 17 knots
B. 15 to 23 knots
C. 25 to 33 knots
D. 35 to 40 knots

36. Between November, 1942, and November, 1943, the U.S. lost no aircraft carriers in battle. This was because:

A. There were no major carrier battles during that time
B. U.S. carriers were only used in hit-and-run operations in that period
C. Both American and Japanese fleets had suffered serious losses, and both were repairing existing ships and building new ones as fast as possible
D. All of the above

37. The Japanese flagship in the Pearl Harbor attack flew the same flag from her mast that had flown on Admiral Togo's ship at the Japanese victories at Port Arthur and Tsushima in the Russo-Japanese War. The 1941 flagship was:

A. *Akagi*
B. *Hiryu*
C. *Kaga*
D. *Soryu*

American carriers varied greatly in size and capacity. The two best-known classes were the *Essex*-class and *Lexington*-class. Match each with its size and capability:

38. ___ *Essex*-class
39. ___ *Lexington*-class

A. 27,000 tons, 90-100 aircraft aboard
B. 10,000 tons, 33 aircraft aboard

— Netherlands Ministry of Defense (Navy)

40. The Allies' cruiser line passes survivors of the Dutch destroyer HNMS *Kortenaer* during The Battle of the Java Sea. The flagship, first in line, is the:

A. USS *Houston*
B. HNMS *DeRuyter*
C. HNMS *Java*
D. HMS *Exeter*
E. HMAS *Perth*

Naval Power Answer Key

1. B	9. D	17. D	25. D	33. B
2. A	10. C	18. B	26. C	34. D
3. B	11. D	19. B	27. A	35. C
4. B	12. A	20. D	28. C	36. D
5. A	13. D	21. C	29. C	37. A
6. C	14. E	22. D	30. B	38. A
7. D	15. C	23. A	31. B	39. B
8. E	16. D	24. B	32. E	40. B

Air Power

The dust from their propellers stained the tears
on our cheeks.

*Japanese woman who watched
Kamikaze pilots taking off*

*From the surprise attack on Pearl Harbor which brought the U.S. into
the war, to the devastating atomic bombing of Hiroshima and Nagasaki,
air power was a vital part of World War II. Aircraft carriers and island-
based aircraft projected air power over vast areas of the Pacific. The
Japanese ideal of dying for the Emperor culminated in the Kamikaze
(Divine Wind) attacks by aircraft which dove onto Allied warships with
the intention of trading one Japanese aircraft and life for an Allied warship
and many lives.*

1. Which general promised FDR that, with 12 heavy bombers, 30 medium
bombers, and 105 modern fighters, he could defeat Japan?

A. General H.H. "Hap" Arnold
B. General Claire Lee Chennault
C. General George Kenney
D. General Curtis LeMay

2. In 1940, the U.S. Navy could muster 1,194 combat aircraft of all types,
some obsolete. By 1945 this force had grown immensely, and consisted of:

A. Over 16,000 combat planes
B. Nearly 19,000 combat planes
C. About 26,000 combat planes
D. Over 29,000 combat planes

3. Col. Jimmy Doolittle led a force of 16 Army B-25 bombers on a daring raid on Tokyo from a carrier in the Pacific. The aircraft carrier was the:

A. *Wasp*
B. *Hornet*
C. *Enterprise*
D. *Lexington*

4. The B-25 Mitchells used in the Tokyo raid were specially equipped with:

A. Extra fuel tanks which added nearly 40% more capacity
B. Fake tail guns made from broomsticks painted black
C. A handmade bombsight, similar to rifle iron sights, made of materials costing 20 cents
D. More powerful engines to enable the bombers to outrun any Japanese fighter encountered
E. All of the above
F. A through C above

5. The Royal Navy's two capital ships in the Pacific, HMS *Repulse* and HMS *Prince of Wales* were sunk by Japanese aircraft off the coast of Malaya. The attacking aircraft were:

A. Horizontal bombers
B. Dive bombers
C. Torpedo bombers
D. All of the above
E. A and C only
F. B and C only

6. The Japanese retaliated for the Doolittle bombing raid on Tokyo by:

A. Torturing the captured American fliers, and summarily executing four of them
B. Killing 250,000 Chinese in retaliation against the Chinese who harbored the aircrews
C. Accepting Admiral Yamamoto's plan for an attack on Midway. Ironically, the Japanese were beaten by the same task force that supported the Doolittle raid
D. All of the above

7. The first B-29 bombing attack on the Japanese homeland was on the Imperial Iron and Steel Works at Yawata. The bombers took off from:

A. Saipan on July 18, 1944
B. China on August 20, 1944
C. Iwo Jima on November 28, 1944
D. Tinian on December 2, 1944

8. At first, the Army Air Force B-29's hit precision targets in daylight, flying tight high-altitude formations. They soon changed to:

A. Low-altitude attacks on cities
B. Incendiaries rather than high-explosive bombs
C. RAF-style bomber streams, instead of formations
D. Night attacks
E. All of the above
F. A, B, and D only
G. B and C only

9. From May 23 to 25, 1945, Boeing bombers destroyed most of Tokyo. What tonnage of bombs did they drop?

A. About 4,000 tons
B. Just over 5,000 tons
C. Nearly 7,000 tons
D. Over 9,000 tons

10. Over two-thirds of the Japanese aircraft destroyed over the Pacific were knocked out by airplanes built by which company?

A. North American
B. Grumman
C. Ryan
D. Vultee

11. In the "Marianas Turkey Shoot" the final results were:

A. Probably 400 Japanese planes shot down
B. 5 Japanese carriers lost, 2 to U.S. submarines
C. 80 returning American planes ditched or crash-landed on the carriers after they ran out of gas
D. All of the above
E. A and B only
F. A and C only

12. The American Volunteer Group, or "Flying Tigers," who flew for the Chinese armed forces, had squadrons named:

A. Adam and Eves
B. Hell's Angels
C. Mandarins
D. Panda Bears
E. All of the above
F. A, B, and D only

13. Most of the cargo carried over the "Hump" (Himalaya Mountains) was airlifted by:

A. Douglas C-47 "Dakotas"
B. Curtiss C-46 "Commandos"
C. Convair C-87 "Liberator" transports
D. Boeing B-29 "Superfortress" bombers

"Flying boats," large seaplanes with boat-like hulls as the bottom of their fuselages, were used by Allies and Japanese alike, both as transports and combat aircraft. Which of these were the largest and fastest:

14. ___ Largest flying boat   A. PBY-5 Consolidated Catalina
15. ___ Fastest flying boat   B. JRF-6 Grumman Goose
    C. Kawanishi H8K1-H8K4 (02) Emily
    D. Martin XPB2M-1 Mars

16. Major General George C. Kenney, commander of the U.S. Fifth Air Force in the Southwest Pacific, was a great innovator. He was a pioneer in using:

A. Skip bombing of ships
B. "Parafrags," fragmentation bombs attached to parachutes
C. Phosphorus bombs
D. Large-scale paradrops of supplies
E. All of the above

17. The first intact, flyable Mitsubishi "Zero" fighter obtained by the Allies:

A. Was captured on an airfield overrun by Chinese troops in northern Burma
B. Was shot down by "Flying Tigers" in Burma in early 1942
C. Landed in error on an Australian airfield in New Guinea in June, 1942
D. Crashed on an Aleutian island in June, 1942

18. Japanese Kamikaze (Divine Wind) pilot tactics included:

A. Approaching the fleet just behind returning Allied carrier planes
B. Arriving at twilight, over the dark horizon
C. Flying at low altitude, then climbing and diving onto the target
D. B and C above
E. All of the above

In addition to a wide variety of Japanese Navy and Army aircraft, "special attack" suicide vehicles included boats, rockets, and tiny submarines, in effect, human torpedoes. Match the following:

19. ___ Kaiten
20. ___ Ohka (cherry blossom)
21. ___ Tokko-tai
22. ___ Baka

A. "Special attack" (suicide) units
B. Suicide rocket craft launched from Japanese bombers
C. "Fool," or "idiot," the contemptuous Allied name for the suicide rocket planes
D. "Human torpedoes"

23. The first organized Kamikaze attacks came from:

A. Okinawa
B. Rabaul
C. The Philippines
D. Iwo Jima

24. HMAS *Australia,* which was equipped with fewer antiaircraft guns than comparable U.S. warships, was a prime target for Kamikazes, and finally put out of action entirely. Between October 21, 1944, and January 8, 1945, the *Australia* was hit on how many separate days?

A. 3
B. 4
C. 5
D. 6

25. On April 28, 1945, a Kamikaze slammed into a U.S. hospital ship, killing 29 U.S. Army nurses, among others. The unfortunate ship was the:

A. *Hope*
B. *Comfort*
C. *Solace*
D. *Repose*

26. General Tominaga, commander of the Japanese 4th Army in the Philippines, urged his fliers to make suicide attacks, and swore he would take the last plane himself. He took the last plane, and:

A. Crashed while taking off
B. Finding no suitable target, he returned to base, where he committed suicide in the shadow of his aircraft
C. Fled to Formosa without permission, then commanded a division in Manchuria
D. Crashed his plane aboard the USS *Franklin,* causing many casualties and terrible damage, but not sinking the carrier

27. On December 12, 1944, Japanese Army pilots tried a new suicide technique. It was:

A. Attacking American tanks in the Philippines by crashing onto them
B. Ramming B-29's over Tokyo, sometimes bailing out
C. Diving onto the beaches amid the landing craft and troops
D. Ramming U.S. Army fighter planes over the Philippines

Japanese airborne troops carried out suicide sabotage missions against American airfields, destroying airplanes, fuel, and ammunition. When and where?

28. ___ November 6, 1944   A. Tacloban, Tenuan, and San
29. ___ May 24, 1945   Pablo, the Philippines
                                               B. Clark Field, the Philippines
                                               C. Nadzab, New Guinea
                                               D. Okinawa

30. USS *Laffey*, a radar picket destroyer off Okinawa, was singled out by a number of Kamikazes and in 80 minutes was:

A. Attacked by 22 Kamikaze aircraft
B. Hit by 8 Kamikazes
C. Hit by 4 bombs dropped by Japanese planes
D. All of the above
E. A and C above
F. B and C above

31. A major suicide attack by Japanese units took place against American ships off Okinawa on April 6 and 7, 1945. How many Kamikaze planes sank or badly damaged how many Allied ships?

A. Over 100 Kamikazes hit 8 ships
B. Nearly 200 Kamikazes hit 22 ships
C. Over 300 Kamikazes hit 34 ships
D. Over 500 Kamikazes hit 56 ships

Air Power Answer Key

1. B	8. E	15. C	22. C	29. D
2. D	9. C	16. E	23. C	30. D
3. A	10. B	17. D	24. B	31. C
4. F	11. D	18. E	25. B	
5. E	12. F	19. D	26. C	
6. D	13. B	20. B	27. B	
7. B	14. D	21. A	28. A	

The Homefront

Liberty like charity must begin at home.

James Bryant Conant

The war affected Americans at home, too. The entire nation was geared to the war effort. The West Coast also saw several minor Japanese attacks, and the internment of thousands of American citizens of Japanese descent and their families to camps in the desert.

1. The mileage rationing program, instituted by the Office of Price Administration, was meant to:

A. Reduce consumption of gasoline
B. Save wear on tires and conserve rubber
C. Preserve road surfaces better
D. Reduce the number of traffic accidents, and save lives

2. Before the outbreak of war, there were about 8 million family gardens in the United States. By 1943, there were:

A. 10 million
B. 20 million
C. 40 million
D. 80 million

3. The action which ordered the internment of Japanese civilians on the West Coast (but *not* in Hawaii!) was:

A. Public Law 67, 83rd Congress
B. U.S. vs. Sakura (Supreme Court case)
C. Executive Order 9066
D. U.S. Army General Order 1942-226.5

4. In September, 1942, a Yokosuka E14Y1 "Glen" floatplane, launched by a surfaced Japanese submarine off the Pacific coast, dropped light bombs starting minor forest fires in the mountains near the coast of:

A. California
B. Oregon
C. Washington
D. British Columbia

5. Also in 1942, a Japanese submarine lobbed several shells from its deck gun onto an oil refinery in California at:

A. Santa Barbara
B. Santa Clara
C. Santa Cruz
D. Santa Rosa

6. The most widespread yet least known attacks by Japan on the United States were the balloon bomb attacks. The Japanese launched over 9,000 paper or silk-and-rubber balloons into the atmosphere in the hopes that they would reach North America on the prevailing winds and wreak havoc with their explosive and incendiary bombs. How many bombs are estimated to have reached the United States and Canada?

A. About 50
B. About 150
C. About 500
D. About 1,000

7. What damage did they cause?

A. The death of 5 children and a woman on a church outing in Oregon
B. Two small brush fires
C. Brief power loss at the Hanford, Washington atomic power plant which produced materials for the atomic bomb
D. All of the above
E. A and B only

8. The Japanese government ended the balloon bomb campaign in May, 1945 because:

A. The scarce supplies of rubber, paper, silk, and glue were more urgently needed elsewhere
B. American B-29's had damaged the plant where hydrogen was produced for the balloons
C. Earthquakes and landslides in the balloon launching areas made the operations too hazardous
D. The American press and military kept the landing incidents so secret that the Japanese thought the program was a failure
E. All of the above
F. B and D above

9. The 1942 popular song "Praise the Lord and Pass the Ammunition" was based on the actual words of:

A. A Navy chaplain on a ship during the Pearl Harbor attack
B. An Army chaplain on Corregidor
C. A Navy chaplain on Wake Island with the Marines
D. An American missionary who served alongside the "Flying Tigers" in China

Three books written during the war by participants (either servicemen or correspondents) were very popular both during the war and after. Match each book with its author:

10. ___ *Thirty Seconds Over Tokyo*   A. Lt. Col. Robert L. Scott
11. ___ *God Is My Co-Pilot*   B. Lt. Ted Lawson (with Robert Considine)
12. ___ *Guadalcanal Diary*   C. Richard Tregaskis

The Homefront Answer Key

1. B	7. D
2. B	8. D
3. C	9. A*
4. B	10. B
5. A	11. A
6. D	12. C

*Probably Chaplain Forgy aboard the USS New Orleans

Pacific Islands

I wish the novelists who write about the islands we are passing would say a little more about the heat and perspiration, and a little less about the waving palms and the dusky queens.

Alfred Viscount Northcliffe
My Journey Round the World, 1923

The Pacific Ocean was full of islands, some belonging to the British, Australians, and Americans, others belonging to the Japanese. The importance of these bits of land in a vast ocean as bases for men, ships, and airplanes caused them to be hotly contested. First, the Japanese invaded islands belonging to the Allies; later, the Allies struck back.

1. The first American offensive in World War II was the landing of Marines on:

A. Tarawa
B. Guadalcanal
C. Bougainville
D. Java

2. Wake Island, which was finally overrun by the Japanese, was defended by a garrison of Marines and fighter planes of VMF-211. How many men and planes?

A. 100 Marines and 4 F4F Wildcat fighters
B. 400 Marines and 12 Wildcats
C. 1,000 Marines and 36 Wildcats
D. 1,400 Marines and 22 Wildcat fighters

3. The 76-hour assault on Tarawa atoll (including Betio island) was very costly, and shocked the American public when casualty figures were revealed. What were American casualties on the first day?

A. 1,000 of 5,000 Marines became casualties
B. 1,500 of 5,000
C. 2,000 of 5,000
D. 2,500 of 5,000

4. For the whole Tarawa campaign, U.S. casualties were:

A. Over 500 dead, nearly 1,900 wounded
B. Nearly 750 dead, nearly 1,500 wounded
C. Over 1,000 dead, nearly 2,400 wounded
D. Over 1,500 dead, nearly 2,000 wounded

5. A number of small Pacific islands, especially in the Guadalcanal area, had Allied "coastwatchers" who observed Japanese movements and rescued downed Allied fliers, aided in both activities by native islanders. These coastwatchers were mostly:

A. American
B. British
C. Australian
D. Dutch

6. The Iwo Jima landings, and the final capture of the island from the Japanese resulted in nearly 25,000 Marine and Navy casualties. Later, a number of crippled B-29's made emergency landings on the Iwo airstrip, saving their crews who would otherwise have gone "in the drink." How many B-29 crewmen were thus saved?

A. Over 15,000
B. Nearly 20,000
C. Nearly 25,000
D. Over 30,000

7. "Bloody Nose Ridge" was a hotly contested island feature known locally as Umburbrogol. On which island?

A. Guadalcanal
B. Tarawa
C. Okinawa
D. Peleliu

8. The first Medal of Honor won by a U.S. Marine in World War II was posthumously awarded to 1st Lt. George Cannon for valor on:

A. Wake Island
B. Midway
C. Guadalcanal
D. Oahu

9. One particular island was the site of more actions leading to the Medal of Honor than any other. It was:

A. Okinawa
B. Luzon
C. Leyte
D. Iwo Jima

10. The Japanese thought the island of Tinian, with its sharp cliffs, was impenetrable. The Marines surprised the Japanese by:

A. Scaling the cliffs in the middle of the night
B. Tunneling through the narrow cliffs to the other side
C. Landing on two tiny, undefended beaches
D. Landing on the islands after the Navy shattered the cliffs by gunfire from ships

Both the Japanese and American commanders on Okinawa died on the island. How did each meet his end?

11. ___ Lt. Gen. Mitsuru Ushijima
12. ___ Gen. Simon Buckner

A. Killed by enemy artillery
B. Shot by own men in error
C. Committed suicide
D. Strafed by U.S. aircraft

13. The largest amphibious operation in the Pacific, which saw the amassing of over 1,200 ships, over 500 carrier aircraft, and over 180,000 U.S. Army soldiers and U.S. Marines, was mounted against which island? (Hint: This action saw the first appearance of the Pacific Fleet of the Royal Navy).

A. Luzon
B. Leyte
C. Formosa (Taiwan)
D. Okinawa

14. The commander of Allied ground forces in the Southwest Pacific was:

A. General George Kenney (American)
B. General Sir Thomas Blamey (Australian)
C. Admiral Lord Louis Mountbatten (British)
D. General Hein Ter Poorten (Dutch)

15. Ulithi Atoll, in the Carolines 60 miles from Yap, was:

A. The largest Japanese naval base to be by-passed until the war's end
B. The major U.S. Navy repair and supply base in most of the Pacific late in the war
C. The site of a successful Japanese "human torpedo" attack
D. Found unsuitable as a naval base after reconnaissance by Navy underwater demolition teams
E. B and C above

16. The Japanese defenders of Okinawa decided to:

A. Destroy the American landing forces before they landed
B. Wipe out the Americans on the beaches
C. Allow the Americans to land almost unopposed, then defeat them inland
D. Abandon the island before the Americans arrived

Pacific Islands Answer Key

1. B	7. D	13. D
2. B	8. B	14. B
3. B	9. D	15. E
4. C	10. C	16. C
5. C	11. C	
6. C	12. A	

Weapons
and Devices

I would suggest, sir, that if you have to take any more torpedoes, you take 'em on the starboard side.

Cmdr. H.R. Healey, to Capt. Frederick R. Sherman, aboard stricken USS Lexington (Healey died; the ship sank.)

1. The Japanese 50mm "knee mortar" was small and had a curved base. This weapon:

A. Could be aimed by moving one's knee from side to side when the mortar rested on it
B. Was meant to be hand-held, but rested on the ground, and would break the user's leg if held on the knee or thigh
C. Was actually a grenade discharger, and not, technically, a mortar
D. Had no safety, and was lanyard-fired
E. All of the above
F. B, C, and D above

2. The Brodie device, known to the Navy as Brodie Gear, was designed to:

A. Allow an Army L-4 spotter plane to land and take off via a cable strung alongside an LST, or between two poles on the ground
B. Permit M-4 Sherman tanks to wade ashore across reefs without flooding the engine
C. Launch depth charges farther than before so as not to endanger the vessel doing the launching
D. Improve antiaircraft defenses aboard ship by controlling all guns from a central fire control station

The most widely-used 20mm and 40mm automatic guns, used aboard aircraft, ships, and on ground mounts by both Allies and Axis, were, ironically, designed in neutral countries. Which was which?

3. ___ Bofors (40mm)   A. Designed in Switzerland
4. ___ Oerlikon (20mm)   B. Designed in Sweden

5. Japanese anti-tank teams used a number of methods to attack Allied tanks. Among them were:

A. Men carrying pole-mounted explosive charges which were thrust against the tank
B. Men carrying poles with which they jammed the tank's wheels or treads
C. Men carrying satchel charges which they detonated when they leaped under or onto tanks
D. Men in foxholes with aircraft bombs which they detonated as the tank passed overhead
E. All of the above
F. All except A above

6. The standard Japanese rifle and machine gun caliber was changed, beginning in 1939 from:

A. 5.5mm to 6.7mm
B. 6.5mm to 7.7mm
C. 7.92mm to 6.5mm
D. 7.7mm to 5.5mm

7. The "Thach Weave" was:

A. A special fire-resistant cloth used in the construction of fire-fighters' outfits aboard carriers
B. A large triangular bandage used especially for burn victims
C. A flying formation used by Navy pilots in the Pacific
D. The zig-zag course used by Navy warships where the presence of Japanese submarines was suspected

8. Japanese Army pilots marked their aircraft, to show victories over enemy aircraft, with stylized pictures of:

A. Aircraft silhouettes
B. Daisies, cherry blossoms, or chrysanthemums
C. Stars
D. Birds or birds' wings
E. All of the above
F. B and C only

9. The first Australian-designed and built aircraft, the product of Commonwealth Aircraft, used in combat was the:

A. CA-12 or 13 Boomerang
B. CA-1 Wirraway
C. CA-4 Woomera
D. CA-2 Kookaburra

10. Single-engine Allied aircraft operating in the Southwest Pacific area after September, 1943, bore distinctive markings consisting of:

A. Red wing tips and engine cowlings
B. All-white tails and wing leading edges
C. Large yellow bands around wings and rear fuselage
D. All-silver surfaces, with dull black tails

11.A "Kenney cocktail" was:

A. A droppable wing tank loaded with napalm
B. An aircraft bomb loaded with white phosphorus
C. A hollow-charge anti-tank rifle grenade
D. A booby trap

12. The LVT (Landing Vehicle, Tracked), also known as the Alligator, Buffalo, and Amphtrack or Amtrack, was designed by:

A. Thomas Edison, Jr., son of the inventor of the light bulb
B. Donald Roebling, grandson of the builder of the Brooklyn Bridge
C. Graham A. Bell, nephew of the inventor of the telephone
D. B. Alexander Fleming, son of the discoverer of penicillin

The M-1 rifle, designed by John Garand at the Springfield Armory in Massachusetts, was the first semi-automatic rifle in the world issued as a standard army weapon. It and the M-1 carbine (also .30 caliber, but with a smaller, less powerful cartridge) were produced in vast numbers in World War II, by a variety of manufacturers. How many were made?

13. ___ M-1 Garand (.30-'06 round)   A. 2 million
14. ___ M-1 carbine (.30 carbine round)   B. 4 million
                                           C. 6 million
                                           D. 8 million

Both the Steinway Company of New York, makers of concert pianos, and the C.F. Martin Co. of Pennsylvania, makers of acoustic and electric guitars, contributed to the war effort. Each produced: (Two answers for each question)

15. ___ Steinway   A. Cabinets for electronic gear
16. ___ Martin   B. The "GI Piano"
                     C. Electric and electronic equipment
                     D. Major components of the Waco glider

Allied amphibious operations were made easier by the amphibious truck DUKW ("Duck") and GPA Ford amphibious jeep. How many of each were produced?

17. ___ Duck   A. 5,000
18. ___ Amphibious jeep B. 10,000
                         C. 20,000
                         D. 40,000

19. Shipping transport for the Japanese Army was provided by:

A. The Japanese Army
B. The Japanese Navy
C. Japanese commercial firms
D. The Japanese Marine Corps

20. U.S., British, and Australian aircraft dropped many tons of aerial mines into Japanese-held waters, including the Shimonoseki Straits and other waterways in the Japanese home islands. The greatest number and tonnage of mines were planted by:

A. Australian PBY's
B. RAF B-24's
C. USAAF B-29's
D. USN PB4Y's

— U.S. National Archives

21. This vehicle is a:

A. Japanese amphibious tank
B. American Stuart tank made amphibious with large pontoons
C. Soviet amphibious tank used in Manchuria
D. Marine Amphtrack

Weapons and Devices Answer Key

1. F
2. A
3. B
4. A
5. E
6. B
7. C

8. E
9. A
10. B
11. B
12. B
13. B
14. C

15. B,D
16. A,C
17. C
18. A
19. A
20. C
21. A

Health and Welfare

Dese are de conditions dat prevail.

Jimmy Durante

1. The after-shave Aqua Velva sold out quickly in the PX's in the Pacific, according to writer James Jones, because:

A. The men wanted to smell good for the native women
B. Some of the men wanted to smell good for each other
C. The men drank it with canned fruit juice as an alcoholic beverage
D. It was an excellent fuel for cooking one's rations

2. Due to the pressing need for ammunition and essential supplies, company cooks usually arrived on Pacific islands how long after the initial landings?

A. 12 hours
B. One day
C. Three days
D. 10 days or longer

3. From 1942, the free world tea crop:

A. Was bought up by the United States, then resold to the British
B. Was bought up by the British, who supplied the other Allies
C. Was sabotaged by Indians (who wanted independence) and the Communist Chinese

4. The "Forgotten Army" was:

A. The U.S. Army stationed in China in 1942 and 1943
B. The Japanese Army on Rabaul, which was by-passed by the Allies in 1942 until 1945
C. The British Army in Burma
D. The Australian Army in New Guinea in 1945

Tobacco was a great comfort to all servicemen. The British and American tobacco rations differed greatly. Ideally, each individual's cigarette ration consisted of:

5. ___ United States ration
6. ___ British ration

A. 20 cigarettes per week
B. 50 cigarettes per week
C. 100 to 140 cigarettes per week
D. 160 to 200 cigarettes per week

7. The Central Pacific "assault ration" issued to American troops consisted of:

A. Hardtack and jam
B. Hard candy, peanut chocolate bar, and chewing gum
C. Cheese crackers, dehydrated meat, and candy bars

8. The USO provided entertainment and recreation for American servicemen worldwide. The letters "USO" stand for:

A. Uniformed Service Organization
B. United States Opportunities
C. United Service Organizations
D. United Social Organization

9. In Burma, transport was very slow due to terrain and climate. In 1942, a casualty there took how long to reach a hospital?

A. Three days
B. A week
C. Two weeks
D. Six weeks

10. In Burma, the number of casualties caused by disease outnumbered those incurred in battle by:

A. 3 to 1
B. 10 to 1
C. 20 to 1
D. 100 to 1

Though most armies called most of their combat soldiers riflemen, most fatal wounds were not caused by gunshot. American statistics show how many lethal wounds were caused by the following:

11. ___ Gunshot

12. ___ Artillery

13. ___ Mortar

14. ___ Grenades

A. 5%

B. 10%

C. 19%

D. 23%

15. Australian, British, and American airmen in the Pacific and Asian combat areas were issued cloth maps and charts (of silk or cotton, rayon, and nylon) to use if they were shot down. These charts were intended to be:

A. Worn as neckerchief or scarf
B. Kept in a pocket
C. Wrapped around survival rations
D. All of the above
E. A and B above

16. The standard diet of Japanese soldiers in the field included rice and soy sauce. Other favorite foods were:

A. Pickled plums
B. Octopus (dried, canned, or preserved)
C. Dried bread
D. Pickled radishes
E. All of the above
F. All except C, above

17. When supply was adequate, the Japanese daily ration varied from:

A. 8 oz. to 1 lb. daily
B. 1 to 2½ lbs. daily
C. 2½ to 4 lbs. daily
D. 4 to 6 lbs. daily

18. *Tsutsugamushi* fever was:

A. Scrub typhus
B. Food poisoning caused by eating spoiled Japanese rations
C. The Japanese name for malaria
D. Dengue fever

19. Scabies is a disease caused by a tiny mite. In World War II, how many GI's suffered from this itching ailment?

A. 50,000
B. 90,000
C. 200,000
D. 500,000

20. On Guam in June, 1945, servicemen preparing to return to the States received orientation instructions including such reminders as:

A typical American breakfast consists of such strange foods as cantaloupe, fresh eggs, milk, ham, etc.
Belching or passing wind in company is strictly frowned upon. . .
The common practice of mixing various items, such as corned beef and pudding, or lima beans and peaches, to make it more palatable will be refrained from
In motion picture theaters. . . it is not considered good form to whistle every time a female over 8 and under 80 crosses the screen
DO NOT walk behind the nearest tree or automobile [to urinate]

These instructions:

A. Were issued by the commanding general, who worried that his men had forgotten all their manners living on the island
B. Were a wry joke typed up by some unknown, and circulated
C. Were a last Japanese propaganda attempt to demoralize American soldiers and airmen

Health and Welfare Answer Key

1. C	6. B	11. D	16. E
2. D	7. B	12. C	17. C
3. B	8. C	13. B	18. A
4. C	9. D	14. A	19. B
5. C	10. D	15. E	20. B

Jargon

I shall return.

Douglas MacArthur

More of that Army and Navy talk with some Japanese and pidgin vocabulary.

Japanese vocabulary quiz. Match honorable words with English equivalent, please! (One answer not used)

1. ___ Kempeitai
2. ___ Dai-Ichi
3. ___ Seppuku
4. ___ Hinomaru
5. ___ Bushido

A. Number One (Tokyo hotel)
B. Ritual suicide (inaccurately called hara-kiri)
C. Japanese warrior code
D. Name given to Japanese merchant ships
E. Japanese secret military police
F. Red disc insignia used on Japanese aircraft

Pidgin English, a combination of simplified English and local words, was the common language of many Pacific islands. Can you translate? (Hint: Pronunciation is similar to Italian or Spanish, and the letter "p" is substituted for "f.")

6. ___ Nambish
7. ___ Kaikai
8. ___ Killim
9. ___ Nambawan kiep
10. ___ Straitpela tok
11. ___ Olman

A. Leader (#1 officer)
B. To hurt, wound or injure
C. Beach, coast, or shore
D. To eat
E. Local residents (all people)
F. The truth

12. The U.S. Marine expression "Gung ho" comes from:

A. The Japanese words for "pushing uphill"
B. The Navaho equivalent of "try harder"
C. The name of a Communist Chinese cooperative organization
D. A Hawaiian canoeist chant

Japanese soldiers, sailors, and airmen often wore special garments into battle. These included:

13. ___ Senninbari
14. ___ Hachimaki

A. A samurai-style headband often worn by Kamikaze pilots
B. A neck scarf blessed by a Shinto priest, containing sacred writings
C. A "thousand-stitch" wrapper, worn under clothing around the waist
D. A symbolic small kimono with one's family crest upon it

15. The Southeast Asia Command, under British commanders, was cynically known as:

A. Swamps, Elephants, and Chiggers
B. Save England's Asiatic Colonies
C. Sufferers: English, Australians, and Chinese
D. Stop Every Attempt at Cravenness

The Japanese names for their emigrants to foreign countries, or foreign-born Japanese, were:

16. ___ Nisei
17. ___ Yonsei
18. ___ Issei
19. ___ Sansei

A. First generation (Japanese-born)
B. Second generation (born overseas of Japanese parents)
C. Third generation
D. Fourth generation

Australian soldiers were informally divided into three groups, depending on how and why they joined up:

20. ___ Rainbows
21. ___ Chocolate soldiers
22. ___ AIF

A. Volunteers (mostly militia) who transferred to active units before the end of 1942
B. Compulsorily transferred after the end of 1942, most stayed with their militia units
C. Agreed to serve only if Australia were invaded

23. Marston mats were:

A. Soft pads to place underneath sleeping bags to keep the user off the ground
B. Perforated steel or aluminum sheets, used as roadways or runways where the ground was unsuitable for traffic or landing
C. Fenders used to prevent ships from damage when docking

24. The USS *Intrepid* was nicknamed the:

A. Decrepit
B. Stupid
C. Dry I (for time spent in drydock)
D. Interpreter
E. A and C above

25. The USS *Saratoga* was nicknamed

A. Sara
B. Toga
C. Iron Lady
D. Gray Ghost
E. All of the above
F. All but D above

Jargon Answer Key

1. E	6. C	11. E	16. B	21. C
2. A	7. D	12. C	17. D	22. A
3. B	8. B	13. C	18. A	23. B
4. F	9. A	14. A	19. C	24. E
5. C	10. F	15. B	20. B	25. F

A-Bomb

The force from which the sun draws its power has been loosed against those who brought war to the Far East.

Harry S. Truman

The most devastating weapon of the war, and one of the most secret, was the atomic bomb, developed by the United States with the help of a number of scientists who had escaped the Axis powers. Only two atomic bombs have ever been used in anger, and both destroyed Japanese cities.

Among the scientists who worked on the atom bomb project, there was a difference of opinion about the use of the bomb. Some even felt that the bomb was too awful to use at all. Who felt which way? (Two answers for each question.)

1. Preferred not to use the bomb at all
2. Suggested demonstrating the bomb to Japan before using it against an actual target

A. James Conant
B. Niels Bohr
C. Vannevar Bush
D. Leo Szilard

3. Colonel Paul Tibbetts was the pilot of the B-29 that dropped the Hiroshima bomb, and commander of the entire unit that trained to drop atomic bombs. The unit was the:

A. 399th Squadron
B. 509th Composite Group
C. 216th Special Flight
D. 888th Bomb Wing

4. The *Enola Gay,* distinguished as the first atomic bomber, now in storage at a Smithsonian Institution facility, was named for Col. Tibbetts':

A. Wife
B. Mother
C. Daughter
D. Niece
E. Godchild

5. The bomb dropped on Hiroshima weighed:

A. 3 tons
B. 4 tons
C. 5 tons
D. 7 tons

There were several differences between the atomic bomb missions over Hiroshima and Nagasaki. They were:
(Fill in the blanks with "H" for Hiroshima bomb mission, and "N" for Nagasaki bomb mission.)

Pilot:
6. Col. Tibbetts ___ 7. Maj. Sweeney ___
Airplane:
8. *Bock's Car* ___ 9. *Enola Gay* ___
Bomb Nickname:
10. Fat Man ___ 11. Little Boy ___
Number of men in crew:
12. Twelve ___ 13. Thirteen ___
Composition of bomb:
14. Uranium ___ 15. Plutonium ___
Was bomb tested before?
16. Yes ___ 17. No ___

18. Nagasaki was surprisingly the secondary target, bombed when the primary target was obscured by clouds. The primary target was:

A. Matsuyama
B. Kyoto
C. Kokura
D. Kagoshima

19. The first atomic bomb tested (before either bomb was dropped) was detonated at (in):

A. Trinity Site
B. Alamogordo, New Mexico
C. Jornada del Muerte
D. All of the above

A-Bomb Answer Key

1. A,C	6. H	11. N	16. N
2. B,D	7. N	12. H	17. H
3. B	8. N	13. N	18. C
4. B	9. H	14. H	19. D
5. C	10. H	15. N	

The End

The responsibility of the great states is to serve
and not to dominate the world.

Harry S. Truman

1. In the campaign against Allied ships off Okinawa between March 26 and April 30, 1945, how many Japanese warplanes were lost (both Kamikaze and regular attack)?

A. 200
B. 400
C. 1,000
D. 1,500

2. The John Birch Society was named for an American who was killed by Communist Chinese a few days after World War II ended. John Birch had been:

A. An intelligence officer for the "Flying Tigers"
B. An American missionary among the Chinese
C. A captain in the O.S.S.
D. All of the above
E. A and B only
F. B and C only

How many Japanese warships were sunk by these Allies, without participation by the Americans? (In other instances, U.S. forces aided by New Zealand, Australian, Dutch, and British forces sank 10 Japanese naval vessels.) Use one answer twice.

3. ___ British	A.	2
4. ___ Netherlands	B.	5
5. ___ Australian	C.	7
6. ___ Russian	D.	28
7. ___ New Zealand		

8. During 1944-45 the United States' attitude towards Ho Chi Minh, founder and leader of the Viet Minh in Indochina, was:

A. To ignore him, since his intentions were uncertain
B. To oppose his collaboration with the Japanese
C. To support him, as he was anti-Japanese
D. To attempt to assassinate him to neutralize native opposition to the French

9. Japanese aircraft engaged in air defense of the home islands were specially marked with:

A. All-red engine cowlings
B. White bands around the fuselage or around the wings
C. Yellow wing tips
D. All of the above

10. The largest all-volunteer army to serve on the Allied side, with a total of 2 million men serving in the Asian, European and African theaters, was:

A. The Australian Army
B. The Indian Army
C. The British Royal Army
D. The United States Army

11. By early 1945, the Communist Chinese forces had liberated 18 large areas from the Japanese (and from the Nationalists). The population in these areas totaled:

A. About 20 million people
B. Over 40 million people
C. About 75 million people
D. Nearly 100 million people

12. President Truman ordered that all Japanese political prisoners be released from Japanese jails. There were 4 classes of political prisoners at various jails on the islands. Select the one below that was *not* part of the 4 classes:

A. Christian war resisters
B. Korean independence fighters
C. Manchurian independence fighters
D. Minseito party members
E. Communist party members

13. Select the location reserved for the detention of Japanese War criminals to be tried by the Allied War Crimes Tribunal:

A. The Dai Ichi Building
B. Sugamo Prison
C. Yokohama Custom House
D. Grand Hotel, Yokohama

14. What senior allied officer was nicknamed "Skinny" by the war's end?

A. General of the Army Douglas MacArthur
B. Dutch General Hein Ter Poorton
C. Lieutenant General Jonathan Wainwright
D. British Lieutenant General Arthur Percival

15. At the formal surrender ceremonies, aboard the USS *Missouri,* who signed the official document first for the allies?

A. Admiral Chester Nimitz
B. General Douglas MacArthur
C. Field Marshall Wavell
D. Lieutenant General Jonathan Wainwright

16. Who was Baw Maw?

A. Tokyo Rose's confidant in Japan
B. Owner of the Baw Maw department store in Tokyo
C. Japanese puppet president of occupied Burma

17. On January 15, 1942, the ABDA Command was formed. As an early forerunner to the future NATO and SEATO Commands after the war, ABDA was the first attempt at a unified, combined command involving several national forces. What did the letters ABDA stand for?

A. All British Deterrent Armies
B. Activated British-Dutch Armies (including Australian and New Zealand forces)
C. American, British, Dutch, Australian
D. Anglo-Burmese Divisional Army

18. The recapture of the fortress at Corregidor, the Philippines, was accomplished by:

A. The destruction of Fort Drum, the "concrete battleship" in Manila harbor, by pumping it full of explosive material
B. Dropping paratroopers on top of "Topside"
C. Starving out the Japanese defenders
D. None of these; the Japanese garrison held out until after the surrender
E. A and B

19. The Japanese sank or severely damaged 19 U.S. warships in the attack on Pearl Harbor. All but three were raised or repaired to fight against the Japanese. The USS *Arizona* remains a monument to the dead in the Pearl attack. Which other two ships did not serve further?

A. USS *Nevada*   C. USS *Texas*
B. USS *Oklahoma*   D. USS *Utah*

20. On the morning of August 15, 1945, a group of young Japanese officers briefly took over the grounds of Emperor Hirohito's palace before they were ousted by loyal troops. They had sought to:

A. Assassinate the royal family
B. Compel the Emperor to agree to surrender
C. Prevent Hirohito from broadcasting the surrender message to the Japanese people
D. Intercept the Imperial General Staff and prevent them from agreeing to surrender

21. The surrender ceremony aboard the USS *Missouri,* was scheduled for August 31, 1945 in Tokyo Bay. This was postponed to September 2, because:

A. General MacArthur refused to be kept waiting by the Allied officers who were to sign, and did not himself arrive until September 1
B. The Japanese signatories could not be found for two days
C. Differences between the European- and Japanese-style calendars caused confusion
D. A typhoon delayed the arrival of the Allied occupation force in Japan

The official instrument of surrender was signed in Tokyo Bay on September 2, 1945. When did the Japanese forces elsewhere finally surrender officially?

22. ___ Korea (at Seoul)   A. Sept. 3, 1945
23. ___ Philippines (at Camp Hay,   B. Sept. 9, 1945
         Baguio, Luzon)   C. Sept. 12, 1945
24. ___ Southeast Asia (at Singapore)

Allied signers of the official surrender document, done at Tokyo Bay, September 2, 1945 are depicted here. Match each one with the letter depicting him in the photo:

25. ___ General of the Army Douglas MacArthur
26. ___ Fleet Admiral Chester Nimitz
27. ___ Admiral W. Halsey

The End Answer Key

1. C	7. A	13. B	19. B,D	25. A
2. D	8. C	14. C	20. C	26. B
3. D	9. B	15. A	21. D	27. C
4. C	10. B	16. C	22. B	
5. B	11. D	17. C	23. A	
6. A	12. C	18. E	24. C	

FURTHER READING

While there are several good accounts of the surprise attack on Pearl Harbor, the most dispassionate and informative account of the planning, execution, and aftermath is *Pearl Harbor: Why, How, Fleet Salvage, and Final Appraisal* (Washington, Government Printing Office, 1968) by Vice Admiral Homer N. Wallin, USN (Ret.), a witness to the attack, and officer in charge of salvage at Pearl Harbor.

Samuel Eliot Morison's epic fifteen-volume *History of the United States Naval Operations in World War II* (Boston: Little, Brown, 1947-1962), and the condensed version, *The Two-Ocean War: A Short History of the United States Navy in World War II* (Boston: Little, Brown, 1963) are excellent accounts of the war, with emphasis on Pacific operations, by the Navy's official historian. Fletcher Pratt's *The Marines' War: An Account of the Struggle for the Pacific from Both American and Japanese Sources* (New York: Sloane, 1948) covers the amphibious landings carried out by the Marines on so many islands.

Good foreign accounts of the war include the official British history, Major General S. Woodburn Kirby's *The War Against Japan* (London: HMSO, 1957-69), and a civilian British account, Basil Collier's *The War in the Far East* (New York: Morrow, 1969). A slightly left-wing Japanese account, critical both of Japanese militarism and the American bombing of Hiroshima and Nagasaki, is by Saburo Ienaga, *The Pacific War: World War II and the Japanese, 1931-1945* (New York: Pantheon, 1978). American views of Japan include the classic *Hiroshima* by John Hersey (New York: Knopf, 1946, reprinted 1981), and John Tolland's large volume, *The Rising Sun: The Decline and Fall of the Japanese Empire, 1936-1945* (New York: Random House, 1970). American aerial operations are best covered in Wesley Frank Craven and James Lea Cates' *The Army Air Forces in World War II* (Chicago: University of Chicago Press, 1948-1955). Volumes 4 and 5 cover the Pacific operations extensively. William Manchester's *Goodbye Darkness: A Memoir of the Pacific War* (Boston: Little, Brown, 1979) is a dramatic tale told by a former Marine who revisited the islands in the 1970's to exorcise the ghosts of the past haunting him.